Science and Technology Policy Institute

State-Level Changes in Energy Intensity and Their National Implications

MARK BERNSTEIN

KATERYNA FONKYCH

SAM LOEB

DAVID LOUGHRAN

Prepared for the
U.S. Department of Energy

RAND

The research described in this report was conducted by RAND's Science and Technology Policy Institute for the U.S. Department of Energy under contract ENG-9812731.

Library of Congress Cataloging-in-Publication Data

State level changes in energy intensity and their national implications / Mark Bernstein ... [et al.].
     p. cm.
     ISBN 0-8330-3416-2 (Paperback)
     "MR-1616."
     1. Energy policy—United States—States. 2. Energy conservation—Government policy—United States—States. I. Bernstein, Mark, 1956–

HD9502.U52S8146 2003
333.79'16'0973—dc21

2003009703

RAND is a nonprofit institution that helps improve policy and decisionmaking through research and analysis. RAND® is a registered trademark. RAND's publications do not necessarily reflect the opinions or policies of its research sponsors.

Published 2003 by RAND
1700 Main Street, P.O. Box 2138, Santa Monica, CA 90407-2138
1200 South Hayes Street, Arlington, VA 22202-5050
201 North Craig Street, Suite 202, Pittsburgh, PA 15213
RAND URL: http://www.rand.org/
To order RAND documents or to obtain additional information, contact Distribution
Services: Telephone: (310) 451-7002; Fax: (310) 451-6915; Email: order@rand.org

Preface

About This Analysis

In May 2001, the Bush administration released its National Energy Policy. Several of the policy's recommendations call for the U.S. Department of Energy (DOE) to explore opportunities and implement programs for further improving U.S. energy intensity (defined as energy consumption per dollar of gross economic output).

At the request of the DOE's Office of Energy Efficiency and Renewable Energy, RAND examined changes in energy intensity across states from 1977 through 1999 as part of a larger effort to identify factors at the state level that have contributed to efficient energy use. This study is intended as a first step in helping the DOE to identify state actions that may have led to reductions in energy intensity over the past two decades.

This report should be useful to policymakers at the national and state level who are interested in better understanding changes in energy intensity and the cause of those changes. Technical appendices are provided in this report for analysts and others who want to delve more deeply into the analytical approach and data used in this study.

About the Office of Science and Technology Policy

The Office of Science and Technology Policy (OSTP) was created in 1976 to provide the president of the United States with timely policy advice and to coordinate the federal investment in science and technology.

About the Science and Technology Policy Institute

Originally created by the U.S. Congress in 1991 as the Critical Technologies Institute and renamed in 1998, the Science and Technology Policy Institute is a federally funded research and development center sponsored by the National Science Foundation and managed by RAND. The Institute's mission is to help improve public policy by conducting objective, independent research and analysis on policy issues that involve science and technology.

To this end, the Institute

- supports the OSTP and other Executive Branch agencies, offices, and councils
- helps science and technology decisionmakers understand the likely consequences of their decisions and choose among alternative policies
- helps to improve understanding in both the public and private sectors of the ways in which science and technology can better serve national objectives.

In carrying out its mission, the Institute consults broadly with representatives from private industry, institutions of higher education, and other nonprofit institutions.

Inquiries regarding the Science and Technology Policy Institute may be directed to:

Helga Rippen, PhD, MD, MPH
Director
Science and Technology Policy Institute
RAND
1200 South Hayes Street
Arlington, VA 22202-5050
Phone: (703) 413-1100 x5574
Web: http://www.rand.org/scitech/stpi
Email: stpi@rand.org

Contents

Figures

Tables

x

Summary

The National Energy Policy (NEP) released by the Bush administration in 2001 calls for continued reductions in *energy intensity,* which is typically defined as *energy consumption per dollar of gross economic output.* This study helps to identify states in which energy intensity has declined most sharply after taking into account non-policy-related factors that influence changes in energy intensity.

The analysis in this report is a first step toward understanding

- how changes (i.e., increases or decreases) in energy intensity differed across states over the past two decades

- how much of those changes is attributable to factors we can measure

- how much of those changes is potentially due to unobserved factors, which could possibly include state-level energy policies and actions.

States vary significantly in how they use energy, which is well illustrated by the changes in energy use by state over the past 20 or so years. In absolute terms, energy intensity varies substantially among states, but the magnitude and direction of change in energy intensity also vary significantly.

Analysis of energy intensity in the United States is often done at the national or energy-consuming-sector level. Because there is significant variation in energy intensity among states, we recognized that having more-disaggregate data could provide a more-robust set of analyses that may uncover additional information on what affects changes in energy intensity.

In this report, we examine changes in energy intensity in each of the 48 contiguous states, and we examine changes in energy intensity in the states' residential, commercial, industrial, and transportation energy-consuming sectors over the 1977–1999 study period. In attempting to better understand the variation in changes in energy intensity among states, we identified a number of factors that may explain why some states had different patterns of energy intensity than others. Those factors include:

- Energy prices
- Composition of an economic sector's output (e.g., the mix or type of industrial or commercial activities)

- Capacity utilization
- Capital investment and new construction
- Population and demographics
- Climate
- Technological innovation
- Energy policies and actions of national, state, and local governments.

The primary goal of this study is to measure how energy intensity varies across and within states, net of the effects of energy prices and other measured determinants of energy intensity. To this end, we use econometric techniques to model energy intensity as a function of four components:

- Measured variables (which we call the "factor effect")
- Fixed differences across states—i.e., unmeasured factors that are fixed in time but vary across states
- An aggregate time trend—i.e., unmeasured factors common to all states (which we call the "common effect")
- A "residual energy intensity" that varies across and within states.

In this report, we focus on residual energy intensity, which is a given state's energy intensity that cannot be explained by observed factors or by overall time trends. We do not know exactly what is "contained" in the residual, but we assume that it may partly represent unobserved differences in energy-related policy both across and within states over time.

We use estimated average annual percentage changes in energy intensity to rank the states in two ways: First, we rank states simply by their average annual percent change in observed energy intensity; second, we rank states by their average annual percent change in residual energy intensity. Thus, the second ranking tells us which states experienced the largest declines in energy intensity net of changes in observed factors.

We show which factors are important to understanding the variations in energy intensity among the four major energy-consuming sectors—residential, commercial, industrial, and transportation—and the variations in energy intensity over time. By examining the effect that certain factors have on changes in energy intensity in the energy-consuming sectors, we can explain large amounts of the variation among states and can begin to understand how those factors can affect energy use in each state. Clearly, energy prices and the structure of the economy are important factors in energy use, and to the extent that states can influence these factors, they can have some influence on energy use. Certain common effects are likely to continue absent any state actions, although, as we show in this report, those common effects differ over time.

We report on the states that had the greatest reductions in energy intensity over the full study period, 1977–1999, and over two subperiods, 1977–1987 and 1988–1999. We show results by total energy intensity and by each of the four major energy-consuming sectors. For each of those sectors, we list the top-ranked states in terms of actual reductions in energy intensity and reductions in residuals. For example, Figure S.1 illustrates the amount of the common effect, factor effect, and residual energy intensity for the five states with the greatest residual reduction in 1988–1999. These states had significant reductions in energy intensity over this period and had annual reductions in residuals or unexplained reductions in energy intensity that were more than 0.7 percent above what we would have predicted after taking into account the factor effects.

We also present some estimates of future possibilities for trends in energy intensity. If the unexplained reductions in energy intensity are dominated by the effects of policies and programs, and if the performance of the top five states were to be replicated in the other states, the United States could reduce its energy

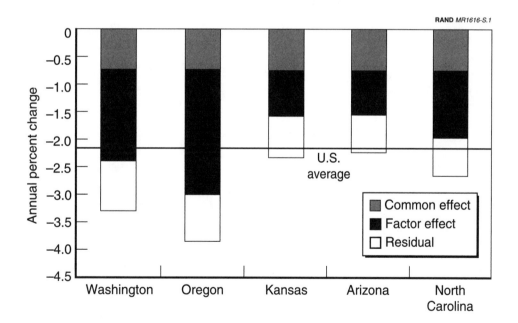

Figure S.1—Common Effect, Factor Effect, and Residual Energy Intensity for the Five Top-Ranked States in Residual Energy Intensity Reductions, 1988–1999

intensity overall by more than 3 percent per year, as opposed to the business-as-usual forecast from the Energy Information Administration of an approximately 1.5 percent reduction per year. The results from this study suggest that there may be opportunities for the DOE to enhance its involvement in helping states share information and provide guidance on effective state-level actions to reduce energy intensity.

Acknowledgments

This work was sponsored by the Department of Energy, Office of Energy Efficiency and Renewable Energy. We gratefully acknowledge the comments and reviews from a number of people who significantly improved the analysis and description of the results. Reviewers included Stephanie Battles from the Energy Information Administration; Paul DeCotis, Rachel Winters, Kathleen O'Bryan, and Erin Hogan from the New York State Energy Research and Development Authority; Keith Crane from RAND; and Jeffrey Dowd from the Department of Energy. We would also like to thank Debra Knopman for her helpful comments, Lisa Sheldone for helping with the review process, and Nancy DelFavero for her excellent editing work.

Acronyms

ACEEE	American Council for an Energy Efficient Economy
BEA	Bureau of Economic Analysis
Btu	British thermal unit
CEI	Commercial (sector) energy intensity
DOE	U.S. Department of Energy
DSM	Demand-side management
EI	Energy intensity
EIA	Energy Information Administration
F	Fahrenheit
F.I.R.E.	Finance, Insurance, and Real Estate
GDP	Gross domestic product
GSP	Gross state product
IEI	Industrial (sector) energy intensity
mmbtu	Million(s) British thermal units
NEP	National Energy Policy
NS	Not significant
OSTP	Office of Science and Technology Policy
REI	Residential (sector) energy intensity
SIC	Standard Industrial Classification
TEI	Transportation (sector) energy intensity

1. Introduction

The National Energy Policy (NEP) released in 2001 provides more than 100 recommendations from the Bush administration on energy-related policy. As part of the NEP, the U.S. Department of Energy (DOE) is endeavoring to identify factors at the state level, including the states' energy-related policies and programs that have contributed to efficient energy use over the past two decades.

The NEP, among its other recommendations, calls for continued reductions in *energy intensity,* which is typically defined as *energy consumption per dollar of gross economic output.* For this state-level study, we measured energy intensity as *energy use per dollar of gross state product* (GSP). By identifying those states in which energy intensity has declined most sharply after taking into account non-policy-related factors that influence changes in energy intensity, this study identifies those states for which reductions in energy intensity have been greater than expected over the period of analysis. Factors that contributed to this better-than-expected performance may have included state policies that affect energy consumption.

Data at the state level provide the means for examining the potential impact of state policies and actions on energy intensity nationwide. If actions that states have taken in regard to energy usage and energy program funding were uniform across the states, an evaluation such as this one would be far more difficult to conduct, and its potential usefulness would be lessened. But because the states differ greatly, including having differing energy policies, between-state variation is likely to a big part of total variation in energy intensity.

Background

Since the 1970s, energy analysts have measured changes in energy intensity as a proxy for energy efficiency.[1] When energy intensity declines, less energy per dollar of economic output is used; therefore, the U.S. economy is said to be less "energy intensive." This does not mean that the United States as a whole uses less energy. It could mean, for example, that industries use less energy per dollar

---

[1]For example, other measures of energy intensity, aside from energy per dollar of economic output, include energy use per capita, residential energy use per household, and transportation energy use per vehicle miles traveled.

of output, or that commercial buildings use less energy per dollar of commercial sector activity, or, in the case of residential buildings, it could mean that households use less energy per person.

From the early part of the 20th century until the mid-1970s, the relationship between economic growth and energy demand growth tended to be constant. But, prompted by hikes in oil prices in 1973, the rate of economic growth since the mid-1970s has outpaced the rate of increased energy use. It is likely that most of the change in the comparative rates of growth was in response to energy price increases.[2] However, other factors may have been at work because even after 1985, when oil prices returned to their historic levels, the link between growth in energy use and economic growth was not restored.[3]

States have played an important role in U.S. energy policy since the 1970s. Some states have implemented building codes aimed at saving energy, instituting various types of codes at various levels of enforcement (Ortiz and Bernstein, 1999). Because building codes require new structures to be more energy efficient than existing ones, overall energy efficiency should improve.[4] States have also been instrumental in working with utility companies to fund demand-side management (DSM) programs,[5] although the level of funding in the states for DSM programs varied widely—from less than $1 per capita to $40 per capita— during the 1990s (Loughran, Kulick, and Bernstein, forthcoming).

Study Objectives

In this study, we address some key questions:

- What were the state-level trends in energy intensity over the past two decades (1977 through 1999)?

- Which factors affected those trends, and to what degree did they affect them?

---

[2]Naturally, when prices increase, demand goes down, and as prices went up, energy efficiencies improved. Therefore, the old linear relationship between increased energy use and economic growth ended, and a new relationship between the two was created.

[3]Those factors, which we discuss later in this report, include changes in the U.S. industrial mix, increased air-conditioning loads, new building construction, and changes in the mix of vehicle types, among other factors.

[4]Increased numbers of energy-using devices, increased building size, and increased air-conditioning loads may make it difficult to see these efficiency improvements in the aggregate.

[5]DSM programs are designed to reduce demand for energy, in particular peak-load electricity, as well as encourage energy efficiency.

- How have those factors and their effect on energy intensity varied across states, and which states have been most successful in reducing energy intensity?

- If it were possible to replicate the experience of the states that had the most success in reducing energy intensity, potentially because of their policies and program actions, what would be the potential nationwide effects?

The analysis in this report is a first step toward understanding how changes (i.e., increases or decreases) in energy intensity differed across states over the past two decades, and how much of those changes is attributable to measurable factors and how much of those changes is left unexplained.

Our analysis should be helpful in identifying those states that have performed well in reducing energy intensity. However, an underlying objective of our analysis is to provide a framework for further research in the form of in-depth case studies of state energy policies and programs. While we identified some significant factors that in part account for variations in energy intensity across states, our analysis leaves some of the variation unexplained. Some of these unexplained differences may potentially be due to state-level energy policies and actions. Unobserved factors, not easily captured in statistical analysis, may account for much of the observed reductions in energy intensity.[6]

Study Limitations

For this study, we were interested solely in addressing the factors that may have influenced how energy intensity has changed over the past two decades. We specifically did not examine other energy-use measures, such as actual levels of energy use and absolute levels of energy intensity. The focus on changes in energy intensity was based on Recommendation 14 in Chapter 4 of the NEP (*National Energy Policy*, 2001), which calls for reductions in energy intensity nationwide. Nevertheless, an understanding of the implications of changes in actual levels of energy use and energy intensity is important, and the DOE should address this area of study in the future.

An examination of changes in energy intensity provides a greater understanding of the issues surrounding energy usage overall. However, there are some limitations to using energy intensity as a measure of energy use. Declining energy intensity does not necessarily mean that people are reducing the amount

---

[6]The analysis we use in this study is based on an approach used in a study of state education policies by Grissmer et al. (2000).

of energy they use because changes in energy intensity depend greatly on the way in which energy intensity is measured.

Energy intensity increases or decreases because of variations in both energy use and economic growth, both of which occur for a variety of different reasons. Sorting out the causal connections between changes in energy use and economic growth is difficult; furthermore, some factors may influence both energy use and the economy, while others may influence only one or the other. In addition, energy intensity does not translate directly to energy efficiency; therefore, we cannot directly interpret reduced energy intensity as an improvement in energy efficiency, even though energy intensity is often used as a proxy for energy efficiency.

Future Analysis

Practically speaking, it would be difficult to examine the policies and programs of every state to assess their impact on energy intensity and their potential success in promoting energy efficiency. As such, we identified a representative group of states (see Chapter 7) that have reduced their energy intensity to the greatest degree and whose policies may have played a significant role in reducing energy intensity over the study period (1977 through 1999). This study was done with an eye toward follow-on research that may include examining these states in greater depth to better understand how state policy can affect future energy intensity. An analysis of state-level actions and policies that may be successful in reducing energy intensity and that may be replicable in other states would in turn help to guide national energy planning.

Organization of This Report

Chapter 2 contains a discussion of state-level trends in energy intensity. Chapter 3 lists those factors that may affect energy intensity. Chapter 4 details the methodology we used to measure energy intensity. In Chapter 5, we present the results of our energy-consumption analysis by energy-consuming sector, and we compare the results for the two subperiods we studied. In Chapter 6, we offer our interpretation of the overall state-level results. In Chapter 7, we report on those states that had the largest reductions in energy intensity over the past two decades. Chapter 8 addresses the following questions: What would be the impact on U.S. energy intensity if the energy intensity trends of the top-ranked states were replicated in other states, and what would be the impact on U.S. energy intensity if all states performed as poorly as the bottom-ranked states? Chapter 9 presents our conclusions from this study and our thoughts in regard to follow-on analysis. Appendix A lists our data sources. Appendix B details the results of our regression analysis. Appendix C describes our methodology for predicting future changes in energy intensity given the results of our quantitative analysis. Appendix D lists the detailed energy-intensity data for each state.

2. State-Level Trends in Energy Intensity

States vary significantly in how they use energy, which is well illustrated by the changes in energy use by state over the past two decades. Figure 2.1 graphs the annual changes in energy intensity for the 48 contiguous states[1] from 1977 through 1999 (starting in 1977 at 100 percent for all states).[2] In absolute terms, energy intensity varies substantially by state. In 1999, energy intensity for each state ranged from 5 million Btus (5 mmbtu) to 30 mmbtu per dollar of GSP. The magnitude and direction of change in energy intensity also vary significantly among states, with the states' energy intensity increasing or decreasing at various rates.

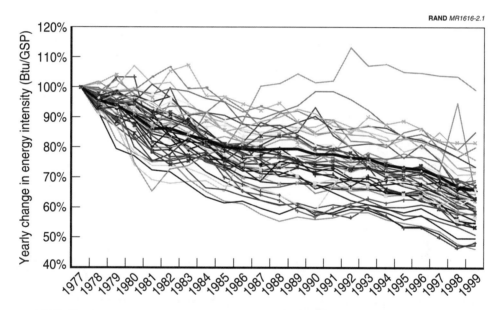

NOTE: The thicker solid line in the center of the chart represents U.S. average energy intensity.

Figure 2.1—Changes in Each State's Energy Intensity, 1977–1999

---

[1]We excluded Alaska, Hawaii, and the District of Columbia from our econometric analysis given their unique situations in regard to energy use and energy prices.

[2]The data sources for the information presented in this chapter are primarily from the Energy Information Administration's series of reports on state energy data (EIA [1995, 1998a, 1998b, 1999, and 2000]).

8

Numerous factors can affect a state's energy intensity rates, and those factors may help to explain the source of the differences in the states' energy intensity over the years. Some of those differences can be traced to lesser or greater increases in energy efficiency within states, but other differences are likely due to, among other factors, demographic changes and changes in the states' economies, including the shift away from energy-intensive manufacturing and the growth of the service sector's share of the states' economic output. Some examples of demographic shifts include:

- the increasing size of single-family homes
- population movement to the southern and western regions of the country
- the increasing size of personal automobiles (i.e., a greater numbers of trucks and sport utility vehicles versus smaller vehicles).

These factors and others are discussed more in detail in Chapter 3.

To illustrate how the states' energy intensities have varied by energy-consuming sector, as well as overall, Figure 2.2 shows the average annual percentage change in *residential energy intensity* (defined as *residential energy use per capita*) in the 48 states from 1979 through 1999. During this period, residential energy intensity declined in 33 states and increased in 15 states.

Analysis of energy intensity in the United States is often done at the national and energy-consuming sector levels. Upon recognizing that there is significant

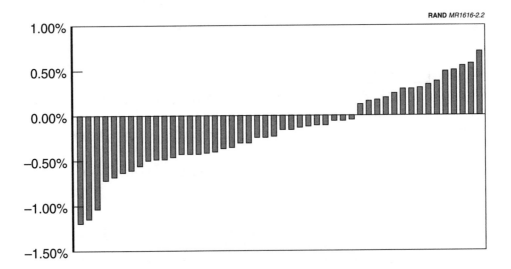

Figure 2.2—States' Average Annual Percent Change in Residential Energy Intensity, 1979–1999

variation in energy intensity among states, we also realized that having more-disaggregate data could provide a more robust set of analyses that may uncover additional information on what affects changes in energy intensity (i.e., if patterns of energy intensity are examined over 20 years on a nationwide level, 20 data points are produced; but if the analysis is disaggregated by state, almost 1,000 data points are produced).

States have not shown consistent increases or decreases in their energy intensity. For example, Figure 2.3 plots the *industrial sector energy intensity* (defined as *industrial energy use per GSP originating in the industrial sector*) for five states whose energy intensity patterns are representative of those of all 48 contiguous states. In examining all the states, we observed a few basic patterns. The energy intensity for some states increased during the late 1970s and then declined consistently from the early 1980s through the 1990s. And some states experienced declines in energy intensity through the mid-1980s and then experienced increases in intensity in the 1990s. Finally, some states consistently experienced reductions in energy intensity throughout the time period of our study. This variation in patterns of energy intensity influenced our choice of the two subperiods (1977–1987 and 1988–1999) used in our analysis.

It can be argued that declining energy intensity in the late 1970s and early 1980s was driven by rising energy prices, and with those rising prices came new state

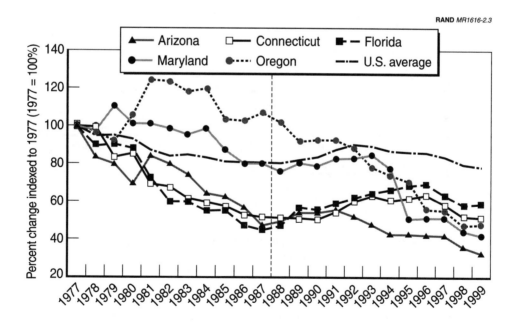

RAND *MR1616-2.3*

Figure 2.3—Percent Change in Industrial Energy Intensity for Selected States Versus U.S. Average, 1977–1999 (indexed to 1977)

10

energy policies. By 1985, oil prices had returned to their pre-1973 levels in real dollars (adjusted for inflation), and energy prices overall remained relatively steady throughout the 1990s, with some brief periods when prices peaked or dipped. Figure 2.4 shows the average price paid for energy (in dollars per mmbtu) from 1977 through 1999 in each of the four major energy-consuming sectors (industrial, commercial, residential, and transportation) and the average price paid for energy in the United States overall. Figure 2.5 shows the average real price paid for energy in the 48 contiguous states, bounded by one standard deviation from the mean.

In this study, we examined patterns in energy intensity from 1977 through 1999.[3] As stated earlier, we also separated the sample into two subperiods—1977–1987 and 1988–1999. The major reason for dividing the study period into two subperiods is that the price of energy is a major factor in energy intensity. Figures 2.4 and 2.5 show that energy prices were less stable prior to 1988—rising and then falling, and for the most part flattening out after 1987. Later in this report, we show that changes in energy intensity did in fact differ somewhat between the two subperiods. Some discussions in this report will focus on the later period (1988–1999) because variations in price were smaller, and therefore the influence of prices on energy intensity was less.

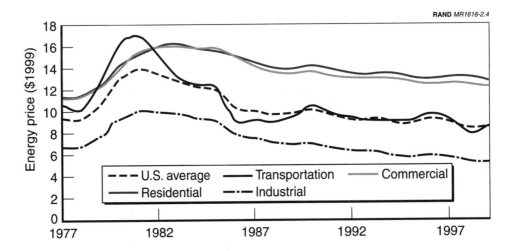

Figure 2.4 —Percent Change in Average Energy Price by Energy-Consuming Sector Versus U.S. Average, 1977–1999

---

[3]Due to data limitations, our analysis of the residential sector starts at 1979 instead of 1977.

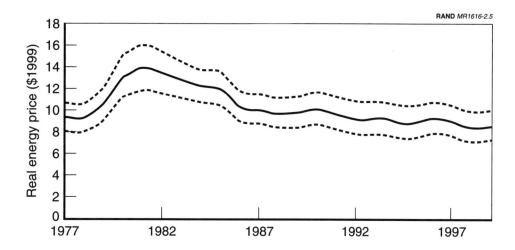

Figure 2.5—Average Weighted Energy Price for the 48 Contiguous States Collectively, 1977–1999 (plus and minus one standard deviation)

3. Factors Affecting Energy Intensity

A large body of literature addresses the measurement of energy efficiency and energy intensity.[1] In this chapter, we discuss various factors related to measuring changes in energy intensity.

As we mentioned earlier, energy analysts typically use energy use per dollar of gross domestic product (GDP) as a measure of energy intensity. In many cases, analysts and policymakers disaggregate energy use to examine energy intensity for each of the four major energy-consuming sectors—residential, commercial, industrial, and transportation. These earlier studies have used various measures of energy intensity including indicators of demand, such as energy use per capita for residential buildings, transportation energy use per vehicle mile traveled, and commercial energy use per square foot of office space, among other measures. Sometimes, the choice of energy intensity measure depends on the questions being addressed; other times, it depends on the available data.

In this report, we examine changes in energy intensity in each state as a whole as well as changes in energy intensity in the states' residential, commercial, industrial, and transportation sectors over the 1977–1999 study period.[2]

Factors That May Explain Differences Across the States

In attempting to better understand the variation in energy intensity changes among states, we identified a number of factors that may explain why some of the 48 contiguous states had different patterns of energy intensity than others. Those factors include:

- Energy prices
- Composition of an economic sector's output (e.g., the mix or type of industrial or commercial activities)
- Capacity utilization

---

[1]See, for example, Schipper (1997); Schipper and Murtishaw (2001); Kydes (1999); EIA (1995); and Dowlatabadi and Oravetz (unpublished).

[2]In this report, we use *source energy* as the unit of measure of energy consumption. Source energy is the amount of energy used in producing energy (e.g., electricity) and transporting it to the end-use destination (e.g., a consumer's home). By comparison, *site energy* is the amount of energy used at the end site (e.g., electricity used to run home appliances).

- Capital investment and new construction

- Population and demographics

- Climate

- Technological innovation

- Energy policies and actions of national, state, and local governments.

Price has been a major influence on energy use, and therefore energy intensity, and the price of energy can differ significantly from state to state. In particular, electricity prices differ considerably due to the energy requirements of fixed capital (e.g., commercial buildings), the types of technologies in use, fuel availability, the ability to move electricity across large areas (prior to recent innovations in electricity markets), and regulatory requirements.

In 1999, the highest average electricity price among the states was three times greater than the average lowest price. Fuels vary in price primarily due to transportation costs and constraints. Over the entire period of our analysis (1977–1999), the price of energy fluctuated; however, over the subperiod 1988–1999, prices did not vary much from year to year, and the real cost of many energy sources actually declined over this period.

The composition of an economic sector's output is an important determinant of energy intensity. Economic output factors include, for example, the mix or type of industrial or commercial activities. These activities, in turn, drive the demand for energy. For example, states with heavy manufacturing as a large percentage of their industrial sector would have a different energy intensity trend than states in which the amount of heavy manufacturing is shrinking. The structure of a state's economy and the differences among states in the composition of their economic output are key to understanding shifts in energy intensity. We discuss those differences later in this report.

Production capacity can also affect energy intensity. Manufacturing facilities running at 50 percent capacity may have higher energy intensities than facilities running at 100 percent capacity because fewer gross dollars are earned for each dollar of energy used to keep those facilities operating. Some fixed energy costs occur regardless of how much use a facility gets, and these costs decline with use as a proportion of total energy costs (although for older facilities, energy intensity may increase as utilization of the facility approaches 100 percent).

Capital investment and new construction can also impact energy intensity. States with more-rapid growth in new capital investments or new construction may experience declining energy intensity because new building structures and facilities tend to be more energy efficient than older buildings in the existing infrastructure. It may not always be the case that states with a larger amount of new construction will experience declining energy intensity, but as the average age of commercial buildings declines (i.e., as new buildings become a larger percentage of total building space), commercial energy intensity should also decline.

Population growth and other demographic factors, such as the level of employment, employment growth, and growth in income, influence energy use and therefore have an impact on energy intensity. As a population becomes wealthier, energy use and energy intensity may rise due to the increased use of energy-consuming equipment (such as computers and household appliances), construction of larger homes, and the purchase of new vehicles, among other factors that change as incomes grow. Because the population and income growth rates vary among the states, these factors are important in determining the differences in energy intensity among the states. For example, the highest state GSP per capita is more than twice that of the lowest state GSP per capita.

Climate also influences energy use and explains some of the energy intensity variation among the states, in particular for the residential and commercial sectors. For instance, northern states have higher heating loads, and southern states have greater cooling loads. Different regions within a state may also experience different annual fluctuations in temperature, and so the effect of climate on energy intensity may vary across regions in a state as well as across states and may vary from season to season.

Technological change can also influence energy intensity. New technologies can make energy use more efficient, but new energy-consuming devices can also increase energy intensity for some end uses. For example, super-efficient refrigerators can significantly reduce household energy use per capita, but increased penetration of air-conditioning into households and the increasing size of homes over the past ten years could increase energy intensity. In most cases, we would assume that technological change would affect all states equally, although state energy policy measures could result in different effects among the states.

Finally, government energy policies and actions can influence the choice of energy-consuming technologies and subsequently affect energy intensity. For example, building codes instituted at the national, state, or local levels can influence how energy is used in new buildings and can therefore impact energy intensity in the residential and commercial sectors. The scope and number of building codes in the states vary widely. State-funded DSM programs, as another example, can promote efficient energy use and encourage the purchase of more energy-efficient appliances.

Factors That May Explain Differences Across the Energy-Consuming Sectors

Energy intensity in the energy-consuming sectors changes over time for various reasons.

Industrial Sector

In the industrial sector, energy use may differ from state to state, or over time, due to factors that include:

- Changes in the industrial mix
- The value of the end product
- Capital turnover
- Improved energy efficiency
- Climate differences.

For example, Pennsylvania's industrial mix has changed over time. The energy-intensive steel industry now constitutes a smaller percentage of the state's industrial sector than it has in the past, which in turn impacts the state's industrial energy intensity.

Commercial Sector

Factors that may influence energy use in the commercial sector include:

- The amount of square footage of floor space in commercial buildings
- Employment in the commercial sector
- New construction
- Energy-related building codes
- Improved energy efficiency in commercial buildings
- Climate differences.

For example, Nevada has experienced rapid growth in commercial office space over the past decade. Given that newer buildings tend to be more energy-efficient than older ones, one would expect the overall energy intensity in Nevada's commercial sector to be lower now than it was a decade ago.[3]

Residential Sector

In the residential energy-consuming sector, factors that may affect energy use include:

- The number and size of homes
- The number of people in households
- The amount of new construction
- Building codes
- The introduction of new energy-using devices
- Climate differences.

For example, some northern states, in which homes were traditionally built without air-conditioning, have seen a rise in central air-conditioning in new and existing homes, thereby increasing the energy intensity in those states' residential sector.

Transportation Sector

In the transportation sector, factors that may influence a state's energy use include:

- The price of energy
- The amount of individual transport (i.e., personal automobiles) versus mass transit
- The amount of freight traffic.

For example, energy use may be higher in states with a significant amount of freight movement.

Table 3.1 on the next page lists some factors that affect energy use and changes in energy intensity. As noted earlier, an extensive body of literature describing the factors that effect energy use can provide further information.

---

[3]Although commercial energy intensity in Nevada is in fact lower now than it was a decade ago, we cannot attribute it to any specific cause at this time.

Table 3.1

**Possible Factors Associated with Changes in Energy Intensity,
by Energy-Consuming Sector**

All Sectors	Industrial Sector	Commercial Sector	Residential Sector	Transportation Sector
Climate	Industrial mix	Number of buildings	Number of households	Passenger transit (mass versus individual transit)
Economic growth	Value of end products	Amount of floor space	Amount of floor space	Freight traffic
Price of energy	Capital turnover	Commercial sector mix	Number of household members	Automobile type and use
Energy efficiency	Capacity utilization	Employment levels	Income levels	Air traffic
Technological changes		New construction	Employment levels	
Government policies and actions		New energy-using devices	New energy using-devices	

4. Modeling Energy Intensity

The primary goal of this study is to measure how energy intensity varies across and within states net of the effects of energy prices and other measured determinants of energy intensity. To this end, we model energy intensity as a function of four components:

- Measured variables that vary across and within states over time (e.g., energy prices, the economic structure, industrial capacity use, investment in new capital, population, or climate)

- Fixed differences across states—i.e., unmeasured factors that are fixed in time but vary across states

- An aggregate time trend—i.e., unmeasured factors common to all states

- A random disturbance that varies across and within states.

We estimate this model using the following fixed-effects specification:

$$EI_{it} = X_{it}\beta + s_i + y_t + \varepsilon_{it} ,$$

where EI_{it} is log energy intensity (EI) in state i and year t and X_{it} is a vector of measured variables (e.g., energy prices, population, output, and other such variables) affecting state-level energy intensity. We model the residual as consisting of three components:

- s_i is a dummy variable that captures fixed differences in energy intensity across states ("state fixed effects").

- y_t is a dummy variable that captures year effects common to all states ("year fixed effects" or, as we refer to them in Chapter 5, "common effects").

- e_{it} is a random disturbance.

The state fixed effects can be interpreted as any unmeasured characteristic of a given state that leads the state to have a particular level of energy intensity that does not vary over time. The year fixed effects can be interpreted as unmeasured national or international factors that influence energy intensity in all states to the same degree. General technological progress could be one such common factor.

We estimate this model using panel data for the 48 contiguous states (Alaska, Hawaii, and the District of Columbia are excluded) between 1977 and 1999.[1] We use the same modeling approach for analyzing residential sector, commercial sector, transportation sector, industrial sector, and aggregate energy intensity. We used ordinary least squares to estimate the fixed-effects models with robust standard errors.

For each sector, we employ different measures of energy intensity and different explanatory variables (see Appendix B for more information). The estimated coefficients, $\hat{\beta}$, tell us how energy intensity varies with these explanatory variables (we later call this the "factor effect"). The inclusion of state and year fixed effects in our model means that b is identified using only within-state variation in the explanatory variables and energy intensity. Thus, the model controls for any fixed differences across states that are correlated with both the included explanatory variables and energy intensity; therefore, the model may bias estimates of b.

While certainly this approach is an improvement over modeling energy intensity without these fixed effects, we admit that it does not guarantee that we have produced unbiased estimates of b. The fixed-effect specification allows for a correlation to exist between the independent variables X_{it} and the state-specific error terms. However, $\hat{\beta}$ will be biased if we have omitted any factors that vary both over time and within states (i.e., any component of e_{it}) and that are correlated with both X_{it} and EI_{it}. We proceed under the assumption that e_{it} is indeed uncorrelated with $X_{it.}$

Although we cannot test this assumption directly, we believe it is a reasonable one in this context. We believe e_{it} primarily captures a number of differences across states, including differences in technological change and energy policy across states over time, and we do not believe that these factors are likely to be correlated with the explanatory variables in the model. The most likely correlation of this sort is between state energy policies and energy prices. Energy prices, however, are determined largely by the global energy market. What variation there is in energy prices across states is likely to be related to geography, which is fixed in time, and infrastructure, which changes very slowly. Nonetheless, state energy policies could affect energy prices through, for example, gasoline taxes. State energy taxes, however, have changed little over time within states, and so the effect of these policies is likely to be picked up by the state fixed effects in the model. We do not think that the other variables in the

---

[1] The time frame examined for the residential sector is limited to 1980–1999 due to the unavailability of data for the earlier years.

model are likely to be correlated with any state-specific, time-varying omitted variable to an extent that would significantly bias our estimates of *b*.

As we stated at the beginning of this chapter, the primary objective of this research is to describe changes in energy intensity in each state net of observed factors, X_{it}, and common year effects, y_{it}, as shown in the following equation:

$$\hat{e}_{it} = EI_{it} - (X_{it}\hat{\beta} + \hat{y}_t) = \hat{\varepsilon}_{it} + \hat{s}_i$$

We refer to $\hat{e}_{it}$ as "residual energy intensity." In words, residual energy intensity is energy intensity in a given state that cannot be explained by observed factors (i.e., the regression residual $\hat{\varepsilon}_{it}$) and overall state fixed effects ($\hat{s}_i$).[2] That is, the residual energy intensity is the regression residual plus the state fixed effects.

By definition, we do not know what is contained in this "residual energy intensity" $\hat{e}_{it}$, but we assume that it partly represents unobserved differences in energy-related policy both across and within states over time. As we discussed earlier, different states have pursued different energy policies over the period covered by our data (1977–1999). For example, the states' building codes differ, and the amounts that states spend on DSM and other programs differ, all of which may affect energy use in the states. We do not claim that the residual energy intensity captures only state-specific policy, but rather that policy is likely to be an important component of the residual energy intensity; therefore, the residual energy intensity may contain useful information about the role of policy in lowering energy intensity.

In Appendix D, we report the average annual percent change in observed energy intensity, $\overline{\Delta}_t EI_{it}$; the average annual percent change in energy intensity due to changes in observed factors (the factor effect), $\overline{\Delta}_t X_{it}\hat{\beta}$; and the average annual percentage change in energy intensity due to changes in residual energy intensity (the residual effect), $\overline{\Delta}_t \hat{e}_{it}$. We calculate those changes as follows:

$$\Delta_t EI_{it} = EI_{it} - EI_{i,t-1}$$

$$\Delta_t X_{it}\hat{\beta} = (X_{it} - X_{i,t-1})\hat{\beta}$$

$$\Delta_t \hat{e}_{it} = \hat{e}_{it} - \hat{e}_{i,t-1}$$

The percentages listed in Appendix D represent *approximate* percent changes in energy intensity because EI_{it} is measured in logs. We average these annual

---

[2]This "produce[s] a state-specific residual that can be interpreted as the joint influence of state-specific factors not reflected in the independent variables in each analysis" (Grissmer et al., 2000, p. 48).

changes in observed, predicted, and residual energy intensity over the entire time period 1977–1999 and over the two subperiods 1977–1988 and 1988–1999. We consider these two time periods separately because the overall trend in energy intensity changed in many states in the latter period, and it may be that the relationship between observed variables and energy intensity also differs between these two time periods.

We use these estimated average annual percentage changes to rank the states in two ways: First, we rank states simply by their average annual percent change in observed energy intensity (see the "Raw Energy Intensity Average % Change" columns in Appendix D). Second, we rank states by their average annual percent change in residual energy intensity (see the "Residual Ranking" columns in Appendix D). Thus, the second ranking tells us which states experienced the largest declines in energy intensity net of changes in observed factors. As we discuss later in this report, the rankings change when we hold observed factors constant. The rankings also change across time periods.

5. Impact of Factors and Common Effects on Energy Intensity

In this chapter, we present some general findings from our analysis of state-level trends in energy intensity over the past two decades. (Detailed data on our regression analysis of changes in energy intensity for each state can be found in Appendix D.) We first begin by presenting information on overall patterns of total energy consumption and the factors that affect changes in energy intensity. We then present our findings on factors that impact energy intensity and their common effects for each of the four energy-consuming sectors. Finally, we compare the total and sector-specific energy intensity changes in 1977–1987 and 1988–1999, and compare the effects that the various factors had on energy intensity over the two time periods.

Total Energy Consumption

The average reduction in energy intensity across all four sectors nationwide from 1977 to 1999 was slightly more than 2 percent per year. Changes in energy intensity ranged from an almost 1 percent annual increase to a more than 3.5 percent annual reduction. Most of the reductions occurred in the first subperiod (1977–1987). From 1977 to 1988, energy intensity on average dropped 2.3 percent, ranging from an 0.1 percent annual increase in intensity to a 5 percent annual decrease. From 1988 through 1999, the average reduction was 1.6 percent, with the range of changes in intensity a bit narrower than in the earlier period, from a 0.48 percent increase to a 3.8 percent decrease.

This outcome would be expected given that energy prices were higher in the 1970s and early 1980s than they were in later years. Table 5.1 shows the factors we measured and how those factors affect energy intensity across all energy-consuming sectors.

Note: In Table 5.1 and in all the following tables in this chapter, a positive sign indicates that an increase in the factor increases energy intensity, and a negative sign indicates that a increase in the factor decreases energy intensity. The factors are listed in order by the size of their effect. Factors listed as NS (not significant) do not statistically impact changes in energy intensity; in those cases, the measure of intensity is energy use (in mmbtu) per dollar of GSP.

Table 5.1

Observed Effect of Factors on Changes in Energy Intensity: Total Energy Consumption

Factor	Change in Energy Intensity Due to Increase in Factor	Impact on Energy Intensity
GSP dollars per capita	−	Greater number of GSP dollars per capita decreases energy intensity
Average industrial energy prices	−	Higher prices for industrial energy decrease energy intensity
Average residential energy prices	−	Higher prices for residential energy decrease energy intensity
Average transportation energy prices	−	Higher prices for transportation energy decrease energy intensity
Energy-intensive industry	+	A higher share of energy-intensive industries within a state's industrial sector increases energy intensity
Heating-degree days	+	Greater number of heating-degree days increases energy intensity
Cooling-degree days	+	Greater number of cooling-degree days increases energy intensity
Average commercial energy prices	+	Higher prices for commercial energy increase energy intensity
Commercial floor space	NS	The amount of commercial floor space is not a significant indicator of energy intensity changes

Given the results shown in Table 5.1, the higher a state's average income per capita, the lower its energy intensity. Or to put it another way, as a state's average income per capita increases, its energy intensity decreases. With the exception of commercial energy prices, when energy prices go up, a state becomes less energy intensive in the long term.[1] We also expect that a higher share of energy-intensive industries in a state would lead to higher energy intensities.

The "common effects" (unmeasured factors that influence energy intensity in all states to the same degree) resulted in a decrease in energy intensity of 0.48 percent for 1997–1999. This common-effects figure means that, all other things being equal, we would expect that all states or an individual state would reduce its energy intensity by an average of 0.48 percent per year.

---

[1]When using panel data, this price effect (or price elasticity) is a long-run effect and does not affect short-run changes in energy use.

Industrial Sector Energy Intensity

The energy intensity patterns in the industrial sector[2] resemble the patterns of total energy consumption across all energy-consuming sectors. *Industrial energy intensity* (IEI) is measured as *energy consumption in the industrial sector per dollar of industrial GSP.* Over the full time period (1977–1999), states averaged an almost 1 percent annual decline in energy intensity; again, the largest declines (averaging 1.7 percent) were in the first subperiod (1977–1987). The second subperiod (1988–1999) saw only a 0.23 percent decline; in fact, more than 20 states had increasing energy intensities during the 1990s, while only six states had increasing energy intensities over the entire 1977–1999 time period. The variability in energy intensity is greater in the industrial sector than in the energy-consuming sectors as a whole. Changes in IEI ranged from a 4.8 percent annual increase to a 4.6 percent annual decrease over the entire period A number of factors, shown in Table 5.2, affect the use of energy in the industrial sector.

In general, the higher the average price of energy delivered to industrial customers, the lower the state's energy intensity. In addition, as the share of energy-intensive industries increases in a state, so would the state's energy intensity, which is the case for most industries. The only exceptions are the glass and chemical industries; the share of either is not a significant indicator of IEI. This may be because the value of these industries in most states is relatively small compared with the GSP for all energy-consuming industries.

Finally, the industrial sector factor that has the largest effect on energy intensity is capacity utilization. As capacity utilization increases, energy intensity decreases. This finding implies that there are economies of scale in energy use, and as industry capacity is fully utilized, it minimizes the amount of energy required to produce output. In the industrial sector, the common effects percentage over the period 1977–1987 is –0.9, and over the second subperiod is –1.6.

Commercial Sector Energy Intensity

Commercial energy intensity (CEI) (i.e., energy used in commercial buildings) is measured as *energy used in the commercial sector per dollar of GSP originating in the*

---

[2]The EIA defines the industrial sector as "an energy-consuming sector that consists of all facilities and equipment used for producing, processing, and assembling goods. The industrial sector encompasses the following types of activities: manufacturing; agriculture, forestry, and fisheries; mining; and construction" (EIA, 2000).

Table 5.2

Observed Effect of Factors on Changes in Energy Intensity: Industrial Sector

Factor	Change in Energy Intensity Due to Increase in Factor	Impact on Energy Intensity
Capacity utilization	−	Higher capacity utilization decreases IEI
Average industrial energy prices	−	Higher prices of industrial energy decrease IEI
Food, textiles, and lumber industries as a share of a state's industries	+	Higher share of these industries in a state increases IEI
Petroleum, paper, and metals industries as a share of a state's industries	+	Higher share of these industries in a state increases IEI
Agriculture as a share of a state's industries	+	Higher share of this industry in a state increases IEI
Mining as a share of a state's industries	+	Higher share of this industry in a state increases IEI
Heating- or cooling-degree days	NS	Climate is not significant indicator of changes in IEI
Glass and chemicals industries as a share of a state's industries	NS	The share of these industries in a state is not a significant indicator of changes in IEI
New capital per dollar of GSP	NS	New capital investment is not a significant indicator of changes in IEI

commercial sector. Across all energy-consuming sectors, the commercial sector has had the sharpest declines in energy intensity over the period 1977–1999. CEI declined almost 2 percent per year over that time. Interestingly, the average reduction in CEI was greater in the second subperiod (a −1.9 percent change) than in the first subperiod (a −1.8 percent change). This may be due to a significant increase in the share of commercial industry in each state's economy and in the total U.S. economy and the large growth in commercial building construction in 1977–1999. The changes in CEI range from an increase of 0.5 percent to a decrease of 5 percent per year over the entire study period. The key factors that impact commercial energy intensity are presented in Table 5.3.

Table 5.3

Observed Effect of Factors on Changes in Energy Intensity: Commercial Sector

Factor	Change in Energy Intensity Due to Increase in Factor	Impact on Energy Intensity
Retail trade as a share of a state's commercial sector activity	–	Higher share of retail trade in state's commercial sector decreases CEI
Employment per dollar of GSP	+	Higher employment per dollar of GSP increases CEI
Health industry as a share of a state's commercial sector activity	+	Higher share of health industry in state's commercial sector increases CEI
Finance, insurance, real estate, and legal industries as a share of a state's commercial sector activity	+	Higher share of these industries increases CEI
Average commercial energy price	–	Higher average energy price for commercial buildings decreases CEI
Heating-degree days	+	Greater number of heating-degree days increases CEI
Cooling-degree days	+	Greater number of cooling-degree days increases CEI
Floor space per industry GSP	NS	Floor space per dollar of GSP is not a significant indicator of changes in CEI
Education industry as a share of a state's commercial sector activity	NS	The share of the education industry is not a significant indicator of changes in CEI

The commercial sector common effects percentage over the period 1977–1999 is –1.1, which implies that effects that were common across states might have led to an annual decline in energy intensity of more than 1 percent per year. In this analysis, we checked for the effect of various commercial industries' share of the states' total industries, and only education was found to be insignificant. Interestingly, an increased share of retail trade reduces energy intensity, perhaps because stores are relatively low energy users. It makes sense that a larger health industry portion of the commercial sector increases energy use because hospitals and other health care facilities are relatively large energy users. As would be expected, higher energy prices have the effect of reducing CEI, and more heating- and cooling-degree days have the effect of increasing CEI.

Residential Sector Energy Intensity

Residential energy intensity (REI) is measured as *residential energy use per capita.* Of all energy-consuming sectors, the residential sector had the smallest changes in energy intensity over the entire study period, perhaps because homes last a long time and are not replaced as rapidly as capital in the other sectors.

States averaged a 0.17 percent annual decline in energy intensity from 1979–1999, but more surprising is that the states averaged a 0.2 percent increase in REI in the first subperiod (1979–1987) and a 0.05 percent decrease in REI in the second subperiod (1988–1999). It is possible that increased electric loads, including air- conditioning loads, and the increasing size of homes offset some gains in efficiency in the aggregate during the first subperiod. Less variation in energy intensity occurs in the residential sector than in other sectors, with energy intensity ranging from an annual increase of 0.7 percent to an annual decrease of 1.2 percent over the entire study period. The factors we measured that affect REI are listed in Table 5.4.

All the factors we examined for their effect on REI are significant. The residential sector common effects percentage over the period 1979–1999 is –1.1. As one would expect, the more people in a household, the lower the energy intensity, and the greater the disposable income per capita, the higher the energy intensity. More heating-degree or cooling-degree days lead to higher energy intensities. But other factors are more noteworthy. The higher employment per capita factor having a negative effect on REI implies that the more employment per capita in a state, the lower the energy intensity of the state's residential sector. It is possible that as more people are employed, the less time they spend at home using energy, although there are probably other additional explanations for this finding.

Finally, the effect of energy price factors on REI should be noted. As would be expected, rising electricity prices reduce energy intensity. This makes sense because as prices rise, people either use less electricity or use it more efficiently. However, rising gas prices have the opposite effect—if gas prices rise, energy intensity rises. This makes sense because we use source energy as our unit of demand (see Chapter 3). This means that we account for the total energy used to produce the electricity that is consumed. Instead of end-use electricity in

Table 5.4

Observed Effect of Factors on Changes in Energy Intensity: Residential Sector

Factor	Change in Energy Intensity Due to Increase in Factor	Impact on Energy Intensity
Average household size	−	Larger average household size decreases REI
Disposable income per capita	+	Higher disposable income per capita increases REI
Employment per capita	−	Higher employment per capita decreases REI
Electricity prices	−	Higher electricity prices decrease REI
Gas prices	+	Higher gas prices increase REI
Heating-degree days	+	Greater number of heating-degree days increases REI
Cooling-degree days	+	Greater number of cooling-degree days increases REI

kilowatt-hours as the unit of demand, we use the total amount of energy consumed in making, transporting, and supplying the electricity.

In many applications (e.g., water heating), using electricity is more energy intensive than using natural gas. Therefore, the implication of the electricity-prices factor is that when gas prices are higher, there is greater use of electricity, which in turn increases energy intensity.[3] Higher prices may mean that residences that use natural gas would be more energy efficient than other residences, but the shift from gas to electricity outweighs the potential efficiency gains from natural gas use. If end-use (or site) energy is the unit of demand, without taking into account energy conversion losses, higher natural gas prices have an expected negative effect on REI.

Transportation Sector Energy Intensity

Transportation energy intensity (TEI) is measured as *transportation energy use per capita.* Of the four energy-consuming sectors, the transportation sector had the most states experiencing positive changes in energy intensity during the study period. The reasons for increasing transportation sector energy use have been

---

[3]For a more in-depth discussion of source-energy issues, see Bernstein et al. (2000).

debated for many years. In this analysis, we exclude air transportation from the transportation fuel used in each state. States averaged a 0.25 percent annual increase in transportation energy intensity from 1977–1999. They averaged a –0.13 percent decline in TEI over the first half of the study period, but TEI rose in the second half by an average of 0.84 percent. The factors we measured that affect REI are listed in Table 5.5.

The transportation sector common effects percentage over the period 1977–1999 in the transportation sector was –1.25. Demographic factors—employment and income per capita—are positively related to increases in TEI, and increases in average fuel price led to reductions in TEI.

The transportation sector is more difficult to analyze and interpret than the other sectors due to the diverse energy uses in the sector and due to the fact that some components of the transportation sector (such as freight transportation) contribute directly to economic growth, whereas other components (such as individual passenger transportation and mass transit) do not.

Comparing Results from 1977–1987 and 1988–1999

As discussed earlier in this report, the conditions affecting energy use in the late 1970s and early 1980s differed from the conditions affecting energy use in the 1990s. In this section, we present the results of our analysis comparing average energy intensity changes in the two subperiods 1977–1987 and 1988–1999.

Table 5.5

Observed Effect of Factors on Changes in Energy Intensity: Transportation Sector

Factor	Change in Energy Intensity Due to Increase in Factor	Impact on Energy Intensity
Employment per capita	+	Higher employment per capita increases TEI
Fuel prices	–	Higher fuel prices decrease TEI
Disposable income	+	Higher disposable income per capita increases TEI
Trucking industry as a share of a state's GSP	NS	Trucking-industry-related share of GSP is not a significant indicator of change in TEI
Passenger transit	NS	Passenger-transit-related share of GSP is not a significant indicator of change in TEI

Table 5.6 shows the average changes in energy intensity for each energy-consuming sector over the two subperiods. In the industrial and transportation sectors and in the industry-consuming sectors overall, energy intensity declined by a greater amount in the first period than in the second period (in the case of the transportation sector, there was in fact an increase in energy intensity over the second period). Energy intensity in the commercial sector did not change significantly between the two periods, and on average the states' experienced a slight reduction in REI in the second period as compared with an increase in the first period.

A number of different factors may contribute to the differences in changes in energy intensity between the two periods. We can check for the average effect of the factors (or variables) used in the regression analysis (the factor effect) and their common effects. But the rest (i.e., the residual effect), as we stated earlier in the report, owes to the effects of a number of unobserved variables, including potentially state energy policies.

Table 5.7 shows the average percentage impact that the factors have on changes in energy intensity. For example, the factors' average impact on total energy intensity in 1988–1999 was –0.9 percent. That is, if the factors captured all possible effects, one would expect energy intensity to be reduced on average by 0.9 percent. As seen in Table 5.6, the average change overall was a 1.6 percent reduction in energy intensity.

Table 5.6

Average Percent Change in Energy Intensity for Each Energy-Consuming Sector, 1977–1987 Versus 1988–1999

	Overall	Industrial Sector	Commercial Sector	Residential Sector	Transportation Sector
1977–1987	–2.30	–1.70	–1.80	+0.20	–0.10
1988–1999	–1.60	-0.20	–1.90	–0.05	+0.80

Table 5.7

Average Percent Impact of Factors on the Change in Energy Intensity for Each Energy-Consuming Sector, 1977–1987 Versus 1988–1999

	Total	Industrial	Commercial	Residential	Transportation
1977–1987	–2.1	–1.3	–0.4	+1.7	+1.9
1988–1999	–0.9	+1.4	–1.0	+0.7	+1.3

In the industrial sector, the factors had a negative impact on energy intensity in the first subperiod and a positive impact in the second, which partly helps to explain why industrial energy intensity improvements slowed in the second period. Essentially, we would have expected industrial energy intensity, due to just the factors alone, to have increased in the latter period.

In the commercial sector, the greater impact of the factors in the second period would lead one to predict that CEI decreased more in the second period than in the first. In fact, it did decrease more, but by only a small amount (0.10 percent).

In the residential sector, by comparison, the impact of the factors is smaller in the second period than in the first, although energy intensity declined in the second period after increasing in the first.

Finally, in the transportation sector, the impact of the factors would suggest that energy intensity grew more slowly in the second period than in the first, but in fact TEI declined by 0.1 percent in the first period and grew by 0.8 percent in the second period.

The analysis in this chapter shows which factors are important to understanding variations in energy intensity among the energy-producing sectors and variations in energy intensity over time. By examining the effect that certain factors have on changes in energy intensity in the energy-consuming sectors, we can explain large amounts of the variation among states and can begin to understand how those factors can affect energy use in each state.

Clearly, energy prices and the makeup of the economy are important factors in energy use, and to the extent that states can influence these factors, they can have some influence on energy use. Certain common effects are likely to continue absent any state actions, although, as we have shown, those common effects differ over time. In the next chapter, we look at what is left over (the residual effect that may include the effects of state policies and actions) after we account for these factors, and identify those states that seem to have consistent declines in intensity even after accounting for these factors.

6. Applying the Analysis Results to Examples of Energy Intensity Outcomes

The results of the analysis presented in Chapter 5 can be interpreted in a variety of ways. In this chapter, we present some examples of how the data and regression analysis described in this report can be used to explain trends in energy intensity at the state level. We present examples from the industrial, commercial, and residential sectors of selected states.

For each example, we examine the change in energy intensity, the relevant factors, the common effects, and the residual energy intensity. The change in energy intensity is composed of the factor effect plus the common effect plus the residual energy intensity. We are assuming that the residual may include the effects of state-specific policies and actions that may impact energy intensity (see Chapter 4 for a discussion on residual energy intensity). In Chapter 7, we list the states that had the largest reductions in energy intensity over the subperiods 1977–1987 and 1988–1999 and the states that had the largest reductions in residuals in order to identify those states that may be worthy of further examination.

Industrial Sector Example

A general trend in the United States has been a reduction in heavy manufacturing's share of total industrial sector economic activity. Heavy manufacturing industries also tend to be the most energy-intensive industries. Pennsylvania provides a good example to illustrate this trend.

Pennsylvania had an average annual reduction of 2.3 percent in industrial energy intensity from 1988 to 1999, the eighth-largest annual reduction in energy intensity among all states. By comparison, the average change in industrial energy intensity for all states during that period was only –0.23 percent. Some observers might claim that the size of Pennsylvania's reduction in energy intensity was partly due to the continuing decline in energy-intensive industries in the state. Although some of the decline is probably due to the state's decreasing number of energy-intensive industries, after accounting for this factor and other factors listed in Chapter 5, we predicted that Pennsylvania would have a 1.2 percent annual *increase* in energy intensity. Given that the industrial sector for Pennsylvania has a common effect of –1.6 percent (see Chapter 5), the residual (or the leftover change in energy intensity that we have not accounted for in the analysis) is about –1.9 percent, the fifth-largest residual reduction among all the states during 1988–1999.[1]

Thus, even after accounting for changes in the industrial mix, Pennsylvania's industrial energy intensity saw a 2.3 percent annual decline (the factor effect plus the common effect plus the residual). Some of the decline in the state's IEI might be due to the recession of the early 1990s, but some is likely due to improved energy efficiency in steel production. Bethlehem Steel and other companies have participated in the DOE's Industries of the Future Program and have successfully reduced their energy consumption per unit of steel produced.

Other factors will certainly have an impact on changes in energy intensity, and the next step for future analysis will be to assess either quantitatively or qualitatively the potential reasons for those changes.

Commercial Sector Example

We use three states—Nevada, Nebraska, and Montana—in this example because these states had essentially the same average annual energy intensity changes in the commercial sector from 1988 to 1999 (–3.14, –3.15, and –3.15 percent, respectively). Among all states, they rank fourth, fifth, and sixth in terms of the largest annual reductions in energy intensity. Figure 6.1 illustrates the common effect (0.9 percent across the board), factor effect, and the residual changes in commercial energy intensity for the three states in 1988–1999.

Each state has different factors that may impact energy use. Montana's factors had the lowest impact among the three states (0.61 percent), and its residual (–1.64 percent) is the highest of the three. Nevada's factor effect had the highest impact (–1.83 percent), and its residual had the lowest impact (–0.41 percent). Nebraska's numbers fall between the other two, with a factor effect of about –1.0 percent. After comparing these three states, it may be worth examining the actions that Montana has taken that could have helped it to achieve these improvements. In Nevada's case, the reductions in energy intensity have been driven by the rapid growth of commercial buildings in the state in the 1990s (with newer buildings come improvements in energy efficiency). Given Nevada's

---

[1] The residual (–1.9 percent) equals the change in energy intensity (–2.3 percent) minus the factor effect (1.2 percent) minus the common effect (–1.6 percent).

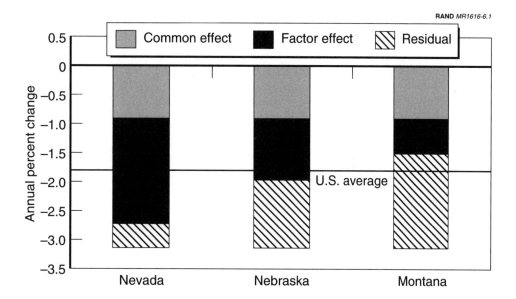

Figure 6.1—Common Effect, Factor Effect, and Residual Energy Intensity for Nevada, Nebraska, and Montana, 1988–1999

relatively high cost of the electricity, the large factor effect may be related to energy-efficiency improvements in new building construction.

Residential Sector Example

For the residential sector example, it is worth comparing the state with the largest decrease in residential energy intensity (California) with the state with the largest residential sector residual change (Wyoming) for the period 1988–1999.

California averaged an annual decrease in residential energy intensity of 1 percent (the next greatest decrease was Nevada's, at 0.75 percent). During 1988–1999, California's residential energy sector became significantly less energy intensive than the residential sector of any other state. However, the factors that affect energy intensity would have led to a predicted change in California's REI of only –0.04 percent. Although it had only a small decrease from the factor effect, California is the only state with a negative factor effect for REI from 1988–1999. (California's common effect for the period was –0.77, and its residual was –0.19 percent.) This example is not meant to imply that California did not achieve significant gains in energy efficiency through its policy measures over the past decade. It does say that there were significant trends that helped California to achieve those gains in energy efficiency, a large part of which were higher energy prices.

In contrast, Wyoming's factor effects would have predicted a 1.24 percent annual increase in residential energy intensity, but it had a 0.33 percent decrease in REI with a residual of –0.79 percent, the highest REI residual energy intensity for 1988–1999 among all states. In 1977, Wyoming instituted energy-related building codes, and in 1995 the state earned a B-plus grade from the American Council for an Energy Efficient Economy (ACEEE) for its residential energy program.[2] Other states with similarly high factor effects did not achieve reductions in energy intensity, so it is worth looking into whether Wyoming has policies or programs contributing to energy efficiency that are replicable in other states.

---

[2]This grade is the result of a subjective analysis that attempts to compare the effectiveness of states' programs to improve energy efficiency.

7. Ranking the States with the Greatest Energy Intensity and Residual Effect Reductions

In this chapter, we report on the states that had the greatest reductions in energy intensity and residuals over the period of our study. (More-detailed information on the energy intensity rankings of each state is presented in Appendix D.) For each of the energy-consuming sectors, we list the top-ranked states in terms of actual reductions in energy intensity and reductions in residuals. We also examine those states with factor effects that one would expect would lead to increases in energy intensity.[1]

Energy Intensity Rankings by State Across All Sectors

Table 7.1 lists the states with the largest energy intensity reductions and residual reductions over the subperiods 1977–1987 and 1988–1999.[2]

The states with largest annual reductions in energy intensity (more than 4 percent in the first period and more than 2.2 percent in the second period) and the largest annual reductions in residuals (more than 0.7 percent) are ranked in order in the table. In each case, there is a slight difference between the last state in each column and one ranked right below it (which is not shown). Although listing the states in this way by total energy intensity reduction masks sector-level differences, it may still provide some insights into which states might be worth examining to further reduce total energy intensity in the United States.

In 1977–1987, New York was the only state that was among those that had the greatest reduction in both energy intensity and residuals. In the second period, all five states that had the largest reductions in residuals were among the nine states with the greatest reduction in energy intensity. However, no states made the top-ranked lists for both subperiods, and this lack of overlap of states

---

[1]This discussion is strictly for the sake of comparison. We are not implying that some states had "done better" than others in reducing energy usage over the study period.

[2]In selecting the "cut-off" percentages shown at the top of the table columns (> 4%, > 0.7%, etc.), we looked for an apparent "gap" between states in the amount of energy intensity reductions. For example, there was a gap between Vermont and the next state ranked as having the largest annual energy intensity reductions for 1977–1987. Because Vermont's energy intensity reduction was more than 4 percent, that percentage figure determined the cutoff point for that category.

Table 7.1

Ranking of States in Reductions in Overall Energy Intensity and Residuals, 1977–1987 Versus 1988–1999

1977–1987		1988–1999	
States with Largest Energy Intensity Reductions (> 4% per year)	States with Largest Reductions in Residuals (> 0.7% per year)	States with Largest Energy Intensity Reductions (> 2.2% per year)	States with Largest Reductions in Residuals (> 0.7% per year)
Massachusetts	Delaware	**Oregon**	**Washington**
New Hampshire	**New York**	**Washington**	**Oregon**
New York	West Virginia	**North Carolina**	**Kansas**
Connecticut	Texas	Colorado	**Arizona**
Vermont	Louisiana	Delaware	**North Carolina**
	Pennsylvania	Texas	
		Kansas	
		Pennsylvania	
		Arizona	

NOTE: The boldface type indicates states that had the greatest reductions in both energy intensity and residuals within a subperiod.

between time periods can also be seen when examining the states' performance by industrial sector. Figure 7.1 illustrates the amount of the common effect, factor effect, and residual effect for the five states with the greatest residual reductions in 1988–1999. These states had significant reductions in energy intensity over this period and had annual reductions in residuals that were more than 0.7 percent above what we would have predicted after taking into account the factor effects.

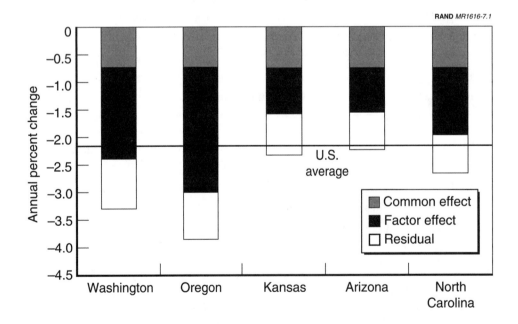

Figure 7.1—Common Effect, Factor Effect, and Residual Energy Intensity for the Top-Ranked States in Residual Energy Intensity Reductions, 1988–1999

The states with the highest reductions in residuals over the second period were Washington and Oregon, at –0.89 percent and –0.83 percent, respectively.

Some of the residual reduction rankings can be explained by sector-specific changes in energy intensity. For example, Kansas had one of the largest reductions in transportation energy intensity over the 1988–1999 time frame. Table 7.2 shows how the five states with the largest overall reductions in residuals rank by sector-level reductions in residuals. Except for Kansas, the five states are among the top ten in residual reductions in at least two sectors, but none of them is the top-ranked state for residual reduction in any sector.

Finally, it is interesting to note that only one state in the first period (West Virginia) and two states in the second period (Wyoming and Montana) had factors that would have predicted an increase in energy intensity. Yet, each of these states overcame the factor effects and actually reduced their energy intensity.

Industrial Sector Rankings

Table 7.3 lists the states with the largest industrial-sector energy intensity reductions and residual reductions for 1977–1987 and 1988–1999.

In 1977–1987, five of the nine states with the greatest reductions in IIE were among the six states with the greatest residual reductions. In the second time period, only four of the eight states with the highest IIE reductions were among the top-ranked states in residual reductions. The top-ranked states in the first period had larger reductions in energy intensity than the top-ranked states in the second period, and only one state, Arizona, is among the top-ranked states for energy intensity reduction in both periods.

Table 7.2

Residual-Reduction Rankings by Sector for States with the Highest Overall Residual Reduction

	Industrial	Commercial	Residential	Transportation
Washington	21st	4th	7th	9th
Oregon	4th	9th	22nd	3rd
Kansas	23rd	20th	24th	2nd
Arizona	8th	6th	37th	20th
North Carolina	13th	7th	5th	15th

NOTE: The 48 contiguous states were ranked.

Table 7.3

Ranking of States in Reductions in Industrial Energy Intensity and Residuals, 1977–1987 Versus 1988–1999

1977–1987		1988–1999	
States with Largest IEI Reductions (> 4% per year)	States with Largest Reductions in Residuals (> 2.4% per year)	States with Largest IEI Reductions (> 2.3% per year)	States with Largest Reductions in Residuals (> 2.2% per year)
Florida	Rhode Island	**Oregon**	**Maryland**
Arizona	**Florida**	New Mexico	**South Dakota**
Connecticut	**Connecticut**	**Maryland**	**Tennessee**
Massachusetts	**New Jersey**	Arizona	**Oregon**
New York	**New York**	Idaho	
Colorado	**Massachusetts**	**South Dakota**	
New Hampshire		**Tennessee**	
California		Pennsylvania	
New Jersey			

NOTE: The boldface type indicates states that were among those with the greatest reductions in both energy intensity and residuals within a subperiod.

In 1988–1999, the top group of states had at least a 2.3 percent annual reduction in energy intensity, and only the top three states (Oregon, New Mexico, and Maryland) had annual reductions of more than 4 percent; the next-ranked state, Arizona, had an annual reduction of 2.8 percent.

Figure 7.2 illustrates the amount of the change in industrial energy intensity and the change in the residual and factor effect for states with the largest industrial energy intensity reductions in 1988–1999, along with the common effect and average U.S. change in industrial energy intensity for those years.

To illustrate the effect of factors and residuals on IEI for the 1988–1999 period, we looked at four states—Oregon, Maryland, Pennsylvania, and South Dakota. Oregon had the largest reductions in industrial energy intensity for the period— more than 6 percent per year, 1.5 percentage points more than the state with the next-largest reduction in IEI (Maryland). Although Oregon experienced a set of factors that could have led to a decrease in industrial energy intensity in any event, of the four states highlighted in this discussion, it ranked fourth in reduction of residuals. Maryland had factors that would have predicted a 1.75 percent increase in industrial energy intensity, but the residual far outweighed the impact of the factor effect. As mentioned in Chapter 6, some observers claim that Pennsylvania's reduction in energy intensity was partly due to the continuing decline in energy-intensive industries in the state, even though Pennsylvania had a factor effect that would have lead to an increase in industrial energy intensity of more than 1.2 percent per year. South Dakota had a large positive factor effect but ranked second in residuals; it might be informative to

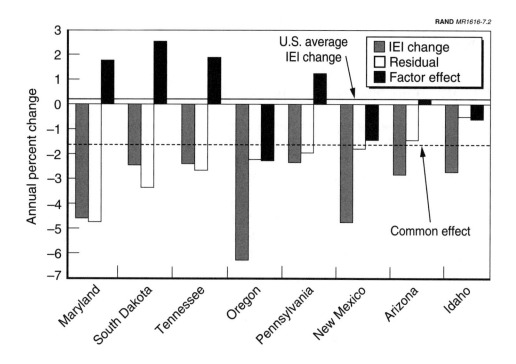

Figure 7.2—Factor Effect and Residual Energy Intensity for the States with the Largest Industrial Sector Energy Intensity Reductions in 1988–1999

try to understand what transpired in South Dakota at that time that caused these results.

The range of changes in industrial intensity and residuals is wider in the industrial sector than it is in the other three energy-consuming sectors. In the second period, three states (Rhode Island, North Dakota, and Arkansas) had factor effects that would predict increases in energy intensity of more than 3 percent. All three states did, in fact, experience significant increases in energy intensity, but North Dakota was the only one of the three with a negative residual. While reductions in energy intensity might be more difficult to achieve in the industrial sector than in the other sectors because reductions in the industrial sector depend heavily on the current industrial mix, replicating programs that focus on improving energy efficiency in the industrial sector might provide some of the greatest opportunities to reduce energy intensity in the industrial sector nationwide.

The top-ranked states listed in Table 7.3 are quite diverse both compositionally (in that some have high percentages of energy-intensive industries and some do not) and geographically. So, perhaps lessons can be learned from the results of the top-ranked states that can be applied to other states with similar compositional and geographic characteristics.

Commercial Sector Rankings

Table 7.4 lists the states with the largest commercial-sector energy intensity reductions and residual reductions for 1977–1987 and 1988–1999.

The commercial sector has less variation in energy intensity and residual effects among states than does the industrial sector. There is also more consistency among the states with the largest reduction in energy intensity and with the largest negative residuals in the commercial sector than among the states with the largest reductions and negative residuals in the industrial sector. Only five states in the first period and two states in the second period had increases in commercial energy intensity, and in the second period, only one state had positive factor effects for CEI. Only three states—Massachusetts, Nevada, and California—are among the top-ranked states for CEI reduction in both time periods.

Figure 7.3 shows the breakdown of the effects for the top states in commercial energy intensity reduction in 1988–1999. Of the top states, the one with the smallest factor effect, Montana (–0.61 percent), also had the largest residual effect. Washington had the largest overall reduction in commercial energy intensity (4 percent), and Colorado had next-largest reduction in CEI (3.7 percent).

Table 7.4

Ranking of States in Reductions in Commercial Energy Intensity and Residuals, 1977–1987 Versus 1988–1999

1977–1987		1988–1999	
States with Largest CEI Reductions (> 3.5% per year)	States with Largest Reductions in Residuals (> 1.7% per year)	States with Largest CEI Reductions (>3% per year)	States with Largest Reductions in Residuals (> 1% per year)
Delaware	**Nevada**	**Washington**	**Montana**
Massachusetts	**Maryland**	**Colorado**	**Colorado**
Maryland	**Massachusetts**	Massachusetts	**Nebraska**
Tennessee	**Tennessee**	**Nebraska**	**Washington**
Nevada	**Delaware**	**Montana**	**California**
California		Nevada	
		Texas	
		California	

NOTE: The boldface type indicates states that were among those with the greatest reductions in both energy intensity and residuals within a subperiod.

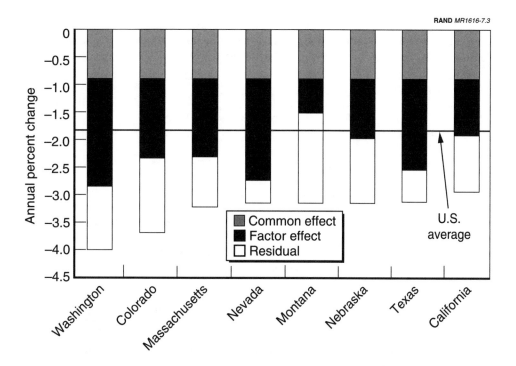

Figure 7.3—Common Effect, Factor Effect, and Residual Energy Intensity for the States with the Largest Commercial Sector Energy Intensity Reductions in 1988–1999

In 1988–1999, the majority of states that reduced their CEI the most, either total or residual, are in the West or Midwest (the lone exception being Massachusetts). It might be instructive to examine factors, such as land use planning and growth constraints specific to states in these two regions, which may have increased the ability of Western and Midwestern states to reduce commercial energy intensity to a greater extent than Eastern or Southern states. In 1977–1987, West Virginia was the only state with a positive factor effect (0.21 percent) for commercial energy intensity. Nevertheless, West Virginia managed a 0.7 percent reduction in commercial energy intensity for the period.

Residential Sector Rankings

Table 7.5 lists the states with the largest residential-sector energy intensity reductions and residual reductions for 1977–1987 and 1988–1999. Changes in REI and residuals vary among the states, but the magnitude of the changes is significantly smaller than in the other three sectors. Only 14 states in 1977–1987 and 27 states in 1988–1999 had reductions in their average residential energy intensity. This outcome may reflect increasing air-conditioning loads and

Table 7.5

Ranking of States in Reductions in Residential Energy Intensity and Residuals, 1977–1987 Versus 1988–1999

1977–1987		1988–1999	
States with Largest REI Reductions (> 1% per year)	States with Largest Reductions in Residuals (> 1% per year)	States with Largest REI Reductions (>0.4% per year)	States with Largest Reductions in Residuals (> 0.5% per year)
Utah	**Utah**	California	Wyoming
Vermont	**Arkansas**	Nevada	**Massachusetts**
Arkansas	**Vermont**	New Hampshire	Virginia
California	Nevada	Washington	South Carolina
		North Carolina	**North Carolina**
		New Jersey	
		Massachusetts	

NOTE: The boldface type indicates states that were among those with the greatest reductions in both energy intensity and residuals within a subperiod.

increasing numbers of electricity-consuming devices in homes. It also may reflect a possible trend toward larger homes. At the same time, all states (except California and Nevada) during the 1988–1999 period had positive residential energy intensity factor effects, so this result would lead one to predict increases in REI. California is of particular note because it experienced a reduction in residential energy intensity of 1 percent per year over this time period. Nevada had the next-largest reduction in REI (0.75 percent) in that period. California is also the only state that is among the top-ranked states in REI reduction for both the first and second periods. Results for the top states (plus California) in reduction of residential-sector residual energy intensity in 1988–1999 appear in Figure 7.4.

Another interesting observation is that in contrast to the commercial sector in 1988–1999, in which almost every top-ranked state in energy intensity and residual reductions were in the West and Midwest, a majority of top-ranked states in residential residual energy intensity improvements in 1988–1999 were in the East or South. When trying to refine the list further, there is not much to distinguish the performances of Massachusetts, Virginia, South Carolina, and North Carolina, although both Virginia and North Carolina received A grades in the ACEEE ranking, and North Carolina and Massachusetts were also among the top-ranked states in energy intensity reductions.

A couple of other states that provide for some interesting assessments are South Carolina and Wyoming. The two states had the highest positive REI factor effects (1.41 percent and 1.24 percent, respectively) in 1988–1999, yet those states had the fourth- and fifth-largest negative residential sector residuals of all states during the period (–0.6 percent and –0.79 percent, respectively). Understanding why

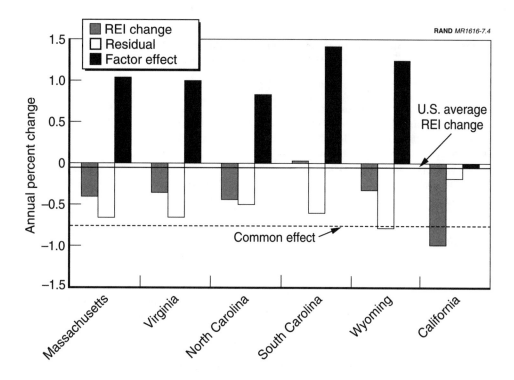

Figure 7.4—Factor Effect and Residual Energy Intensity for the States with the Largest Residential Sector Energy Intensity Reductions in 1988–1999

these states appeared to buck the trend toward greater residential energy intensities may be important to understanding the role of state policy in energy intensity improvements.

Transportation Sector Rankings

Table 7.6 lists the states with the largest transportation-sector energy intensity reductions and residual reductions for 1977–1987 and 1988–1999.

While 24 states had negative changes in transportation energy intensity over the entire 1977–1997 study period, only 9 states had negative changes in TEI over the 1988–1999 subperiod. Overall, the negative changes were not large. Twenty-six states in the 1977–1987 and 22 states in 1988–1999 had negative transportation sector residuals. Texas may be an interesting case to explore because it is only one of two states (Alabama being the other) to show up on the lists of top states for either reduction category in both time periods. Texas had almost no change in transportation energy intensity (positive 0.03 percent) in the second period, but it ranks fifth in reduction of residuals in that period. It is also a populous and geographically large state with relatively low energy prices.

46

Table 7.6

**Ranking of States in Reductions in Transportation Energy Intensity and Residuals,
1977–1987 Versus 1988–1999**

1977–1987		1988–1999	
States with Largest TEI Reductions (> 0.95% per year)	States with Largest Reductions in Residuals (> 1% per year)	States with Largest TEI Reductions (> 0.1% per year)	States with Largest Reductions in Residuals (> 0.95% per year)
Alabama	**Alabama**	Nevada	Louisiana
Texas	**Arizona**	California	**Kansas**
Idaho	**Texas**	**Oregon**	**Oregon**
Utah		**Kansas**	Alabama
Arizona		Washington	Texas
Colorado		New York	
		Delaware	
		Rhode Island	
		Florida	

NOTE: The boldface type indicates states that were among those with the greatest reductions in both energy intensity and residuals within a subperiod.

Figure 7.5 shows the results for the states with the largest reductions in transportation-sector residual energy intensity in 1988–1999. More in-depth analysis, and likely more disaggregation within the analysis, is needed to gain a better understanding of changes in energy intensity in the transportation sector.

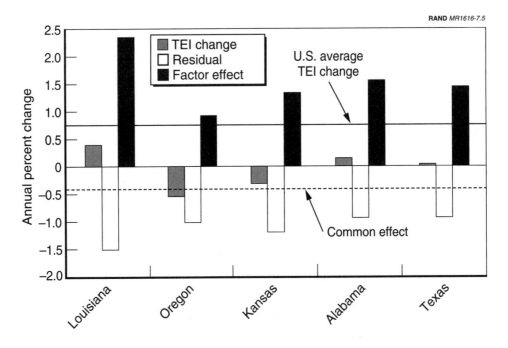

Figure 7.5—Factor Effect and Residual Energy Intensity for the States with the Largest Transportation Sector Energy Intensity Reductions in 1988–1999

8. What Would Happen to U.S. Energy Intensity If All States Replicated the Top-Ranked or Bottom-Ranked States?

In this report, we showed that over the past couple of decades there has been substantial variation in energy intensity trends across the 48 contiguous states and among states within the four energy-consuming sectors. We have also highlighted the various factors that have affected the level of changes in energy intensity over the study period. An understanding of why some states have reduced their energy intensity significantly more than all states on average provides a basis for further study on how energy intensity might be reduced nationwide. This analysis is the first in a series of analyses that the DOE could pursue that will shed some light on the role that state programs and policies play in reducing energy intensity.

With that in mind, this chapter asks the question, what would be the nationwide impact on energy intensity, hypothetically, if (1) all states were able to replicate the energy intensity reductions of the states with the *greatest reductions in residuals* since 1988, and if (2) all states produced energy intensity changes at the same average rate as the states with the *highest residuals* since 1988? In other words, if, over the next 20 years, every state reduced its energy intensity, beyond what the factors we discuss in this report would predict, to the same degree as the states with the greatest reductions in residuals since 1988, what would U.S. energy intensity look like by the year 2020? And alternatively, if, over the next 20 years, every state changed its energy intensity beyond what the factors would predict to the same degree as the states with the highest residuals since 1988, what would happen to U.S. energy intensity by 2020?

Figure 8.1 illustrates some estimates of hypothetical energy intensity trends if all U.S. states had energy intensity reductions from 2000 to 2020 on a par with the five states with the largest negative energy intensity changes and the five states with the largest positive energy intensity changes (see Appendix D for complete state rankings). The solid line in the figure represents the Energy Information Administration (EIA) forecast of an approximate 1.5 percent reduction in energy intensity per year (EIA, 2000). The range below the EIA line in the figure represents a potential reduction in energy intensity. This range is based on our

48

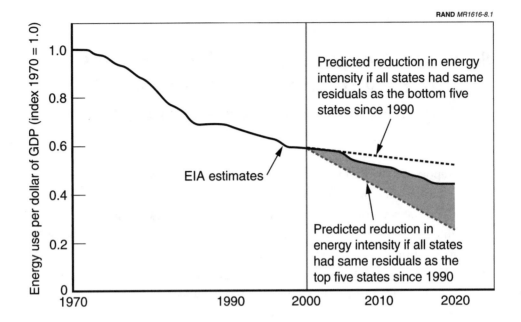

Figure 8.1—Potential Energy Intensity Reductions If All States Replicated the Residuals Performance of the Top- and Bottom-Ranked States

calculations on the potential impact of achieving the same unexplained reductions in energy intensity as those experienced by the five states that had the greatest unexplained reductions in energy intensity over the period of analysis. Some of this unexplained decline in energy intensity might have been due to energy efficiency policies adopted by these states. The bottom line is based on assumptions from EIA forecasts and estimates of potential reductions in energy intensity based on the equations shown in Appendix A. This estimated energy intensity is then modified using those equations by applying the same residual effects produced by the top 5 states that had the largest residuals to the other 43 states.[1]

If the experience of the top states is replicable in the other states, and the forecasted parameters turn out to be correct, the United States might be able to reduce its energy intensity overall by more than 3 percent per year. On the flip side, the top line on the graph uses the same basis for the calculation as the bottom line but instead assumes that all states would have the same residual as the states with the largest residuals through 2020. In this case, energy intensity would decline by only about 0.5 percent per year through 2020.

---

[1]Details of the calculation and sector-by-sector estimates are in Appendix C.

We are not suggesting that these percentage reductions should be used as targets for the United States as a whole, but these numbers do provide some bounds for possible outcomes and might hint at what could be achievable if the energy intensity reductions experienced by the top states are due to state programs and activities that could be replicated across the nation. The estimate shown by the bottom line in the figure could represent a lower bound for potential improvements in energy intensity. Clearly, the trends illustrated in Figure 8.1 should be interpreted with caution, for a number of reasons:

- Certain differences among the states may make it difficult if not impossible for the other 43 states to replicate the performance of the top 5 states.

- Just because a state program is successful does not necessarily mean that it is replicable.

- Although we are producing forecasts that focus on the residuals, assuming that they are primarily due to state actions, energy intensity changes are also due to the factors and common effects that we discuss in this report, and not just state policy.

9. Conclusions and Thoughts for Future Analysis

We drew four general conclusions from the analysis presented in this report:

- Energy intensity has varied significantly among the 48 contiguous states over the past two decades.

- There are differences both within and across states in how energy intensity has changed over time.

- A number of critical factors impact energy intensity.

- It is possible to identify states that have had reductions in energy intensity that are greater than the average reduction for all states.

The results from this study suggest that there are opportunities for most states to achieve greater reductions in energy intensity, as suggested by the performance of the states that have most dramatically reduced energy intensity. The DOE could facilitate further reductions in energy intensity by increasing its involvement in helping states to learn from each other and by providing guidance concerning which programs have been most effective in reducing energy intensity at the state level.

What could follow from this analysis is a more-detailed examination focusing on a small group of states. In cooperation with those states, the follow-on study could determine the potential for translating successful actions in one state to another state and could help to guide regional and national energy policy. The DOE could benefit from learning how state actions may have impacted the factors we measured in this study.

Next steps could include:

1. An inventory of energy efficiency policies and program actions in the top-ranked states identified in this study

2. Development of a set of criteria to help judge the success of various state energy programs—developing a successful energy program is not just a matter of how much money is spent on a program, but how that money is spent and what sort of program the funding supports.

3. Examination of state energy-efficiency programs to evaluate their impact on energy intensity and their success in reducing it

4. Determination of replication potential—this effort would involve determining whether the successes in some states could be replicated in other states or whether the unique conditions in those states generated the results.

Additional data analysis would be required for the follow-on study, including a more-detailed examination of the factors that influence energy intensity and whether specific characteristics of those factors led to changes in energy intensity in the states that had the largest energy intensity reductions. For example, energy end use could be disaggregated even further. It may also be possible to expand the number of factors and further refine the estimates of future reductions in energy intensity. Other statistical techniques could also be used to evaluate whether the reductions observed in this study are trends that depart from expected economic equilibrium or not. State factor effects could also be further examined to determine if certain policies might influence certain factors and therefore indirectly promote reductions in energy intensity.

Measuring the impact of national energy policy and national energy research and development could be another important element of a follow-on study. It may be possible to separate the impact of energy-related technological advancements from the impact of policies and other factors that we assume are reflected in the energy intensity residuals and to trace some of that impact back to federal research and development efforts.

The analytical technique described in this report could also be employed to examine other measures of energy use. Given the limitations in the energy intensity analysis presented in this report, the follow-on analysis could provide a more-robust picture of the impact of state-level energy-related actions, which could be used as a tool for evaluating energy policies and programs across states. A fuller understanding of the source of variation in energy intensity among states can help the nation to achieve further reductions in energy intensity, as outlined in the energy efficiency recommendations of the 2001 National Energy Policy.

A. Data Sources

For the regression analysis we conducted in this study, we used panel data for the 48 contiguous states for the years 1977 through 1999,[1] the maximum time period for which data exist on the variables (e.g., energy prices, economic structure, capacity use, investment in new capital, population, climate) used to model energy intensity in each state. The data are largely from three sources: the Energy Information Administration for energy-related data, the Bureau of Economic Analysis (BEA) for economic data, and the U.S. Census Bureau for demographic data.

Energy Data

Our source of data on energy consumption is the *State Energy Data Report 1999* (EIA, May 2001), which provides energy consumption estimates for each of the 50 states and the District of Columbia by energy source and economic sector for 1960 through 1999.

Energy consumption for any given energy-consuming sector is the sum of all types of fuel consumed by that sector in Btus. In this study, we used data on primary energy consumption, which includes energy consumed by end users and also energy losses from the generation and distribution of that energy. Unfortunately, the data on fuel consumption also include data on fuels used as "feedstocks" (e.g., fuels used in producing plastics). We cleaned the consumption data by subtracting fuel types that are definitely used for purposes other than the production of energy, although we cannot subtract fuels that are used for both the production of energy and for feedstocks.

Tables A.1 through A.4 list the variables we used in our regression analyses of energy intensity in the four energy-consuming sectors and the source data we used to construct those variables.[2]

---

[1]Due to unavailability of data on household size, the time frame for the residential sector is limited to 1979 through 1999.

[2]The undefined acronyms in parentheses in the tables are identifier headings from the source data sets; their meanings were not defined in the sources.

Table A.1

Industrial Sector Regression Analysis Variables and Data Sources Used to Construct the Variables

Variable	How Variable Was Constructed/ Source of Data Used to Determine Variable
Industrial Energy Intensity = Industrial Energy Consumption / Industrial GSP Deflator / GDP Deflator	Industrial primary energy consumption net of feedstocks (Btus) = Total primary energy consumed in the industrial sector (TEICB) less petrochemical feedstocks (naptha less than 401 degrees Fahrenheit [F] [FNICB], other oils equal to or greater than 401 degrees F [FOICB], and still gas [FSICB]), asphalt and road oil (ARICB), lubricants (LUICB), special napthas (SNICB), miscellaneous petroleum products (MSICB), and waxes (WXICB) *Source:* EIA (May 2001) Gross industrial product in dollars = Agriculture and Fish (Standard Industrial Classification [SIC] 10000) + Mining (SIC 30000) + Construction (SIC 40000) + Manufacturing (SIC 50000) *Source:* BEA, *Regional Accounts Data,* "Gross State Product" (n.d.)
Climate Index = Heating-Degree Days + Cooling-Degree Days by Census Region	Heating-degree days and cooling-degree days *Source:* EIA, "Energy A–Z," 2001
Real Industrial Energy Prices = Industrial Energy Prices / GDP Deflator	Average price of industrial fuels in dollars (TEICD) *Source:* EIA (November 2001)
Percent of Industrial GSP from Petroleum, Paper, and Metallurgy Industries	Primary Metals (SIC 51330) + Petroleum Products (SIC 52290) + Paper Products (SIC 52260) / Gross industrial product *Source:* BEA Web site
Percent of Industrial GSP from Glass and Chemical Industries	Stone, Clay, Glass (SIC 51320) + Chemicals (SIC 52280) / Gross industrial product *Source:* BEA Web site
Percent of Industrial GSP from Food, Textile, and Lumber Industries	Food and Kindred Products (SIC 52200) + Textile Mill Products (SIC 52220) + Lumber and Wood (SIC 51240) / Gross industrial product *Source:* BEA Web site
Percent of Industrial GSP from Mining Industry	Mining (SIC 30000) / Gross industrial product Source: BEA Web site
Percent of Industrial GSP from Agriculture Industry	Agriculture and Fish (SIC 10000) / Gross industrial product *Source:* BEA Web site
New Capital Expenditures in Manufacturing as a Percent of Manufacturing GSP	New Capital Expenditures / Gross state product from manufacturing *Source:* U.S. Census Bureau, various years[a]
Deviation from Equilibrium GSP (GSP / Equilibrium GSP)	Equilibrium industrial GSP was computed by smoothing industrial GSP with backward- and forward-looking moving average[b]

[a]This data item was discontinued from the Annual Survey of Manufacturers (U.S. Census Bureau, n.d.) after 1997. Values for 1998 and 1999 were imputed as the average percentage of total capital expenditures from new capital for the previous three years.

[b]A Hodrick-Prescott filter was used to do this computation.

Table A.2

Commercial Sector Regression Analysis Variables and Data Used to Construct the Variables

Variable	How Variable Was Constructed/ Source of Data Used to Determine Variables
Commercial Energy Intensity = Commercial Energy Consumption / GSP Commercial Deflator / GDP Deflator	Total primary energy consumption (Btus), commercial sector (TECCB) *Source:* EIA (May 2001) Gross commercial product in dollars = Wholesale Trade (SIC 70000) + Retail Trade (SIC 80000) + Finance, Insurance, and Real Estate (F.I.R.E.) (SIC 90000) + Services (SIC 100000) + Government (SIC 110000) *Source:* BEA, *Regional Accounts Data*, "Gross State Product" (n.d.)
Heating-Degree Days Cooling-Degree Days	Heating-degree days and cooling-degree days *Source:* EIA, "Energy A-Z," 2001
Square Footage of Commercial Floor Space per Dollar of Commercial Sector GSP = Square Footage of Commercial Floor Space / GSP Commercial Deflator / GDP Deflator	Data purchased from McGraw-Hill Construction Dodge (http://dodge.construction.com/) includes changes in the square footage of commercial floor space from 1977 through 1999 for each state
Commercial Real Energy Prices = Commercial Energy Prices / GDP Deflator	Average price of commercial fuels in dollars (TECCD) *Source:* EIA (November 2001)
Population per Dollar of Commercial Sector GSP = Population / GSP from Services Industries / GDP Deflator	Population numbers *Source:* BEA, *Regional Accounts Data*, "Annual State Personal Income," Population table (n.d.)
Commercial Employment per Dollar of Commercial Sector GSP = Commercial Sector Employment / GSP from Service Industries / GDP Deflator	Commercial sector employment = Sum of employment in the following categories: Wholesale Trade (610), Retail Trade (620), F.I.R.E. (700), Services (800), and Government (900) *Source:* BEA, *Regional Accounts Data*, "Annual State Personal Income," SA25 1980–2001 archive: Total full-time and part-time employment by industry (n.d.)
Percent of Commercial GSP from Educational Services Industry	Educational Services (SIC 100820) / Gross commercial product *Source:* BEA Web site
Percent of Commercial GSP from Retail Trade Industry	Retail Trade (SIC 80000) / Gross commercial product *Source:* BEA Web site
Percent of Commercial GSP from F.I.R.E. and Legal Industries	F.I.R.E. (SIC 90000) + Legal Services (SIC 100810) / gross commercial product *Source:* BEA Web site
Percent of Commercial GSP from Health Industries	Health Services (SIC 100800) / Gross commercial product *Source:* BEA Web site

Table A.3

Residential Sector Regression Analysis Variables and Data Used to Construct the Variables

Variable	How Variable Was Constructed/Source of Data Used to Determine Variables
Residential Energy Intensity (Consumption / Population)	Primary energy consumption (Btus), Residential sector (TERCB) *Source:* EIA (May 2001) Population numbers *Source:* BEA, *Regional Accounts Data*, "Annual State Personal Income," Population table (n.d.)
Heating-Degree Days Cooling-Degree Days	Heating-degree days and cooling-degree days *Source:* EIA, "Energy A–Z," 2001.
Real Residential Electricity Prices = Residential Electricity Prices / GDP Deflator	Average price of electricity to the residential sector in dollars (ESRCD) *Source:* EIA (November 2001)
Residential Natural Gas Real Prices = Residential Natural Gas Prices / GDP Deflator	Average price of natural gas to the residential sector in dollars (NGRCD) *Source:* EIA (November 2001)
Real Disposable Income per Capita = Disposable Income per Capita / GDP Deflator	Disposable income per capita *Source:* BEA, *Regional Accounts Data*, "Annual State Personal Income," Per capita disposable personal income table (n.d.)
Employment	Total employment / Population *Source:* BEA, *Regional Accounts Data*, "Annual State Personal Income," SA25 1980–2001 archive: Total full-time and part-time employment by industry (n.d.)
Average Household Size	Population / Number of households *Source:* U.S. Census Bureau, Population Estimates Program, "Household and Housing Unit" (n.d.)

To generate the energy intensity measures, we divided the energy consumption of each sector by the relevant denominator that reflects the size of the sector, such as the population of a state or a state's GSP. In all of the regression analyses, the dependent variable (energy intensity) is in the log form.

We obtained energy prices from the *State Energy Price and Expenditure Report: 1999* (EIA, November 2001), which provides estimates for nominal energy price by energy-consuming sector and by energy source. It also includes calculations on the average energy price for each sector, which were obtained by weighting the fuel prices by their share in energy consumption. We transformed the nominal energy prices into real 1999 dollars using the GDP deflator as an independent variable in the regression.

Table A.4

Transportation Sector Regression Analysis Variables and Data Used to Construct the Variables

Variable	How Variable Was Constructed/ Source of Data Used to Determine Variables
Ground Transportation Energy Intensity (Consumption / Population)	Transportation energy consumption, net of feedstock and air transportation (Btus) = Primary energy consumption in transportation (TEACB) – Lubricants (LUACB) – Fuels for air transportation (JFACB + AVACB) *Source:* EIA (May 2001) Population numbers *Source:* BEA, *Regional Accounts Data,* "Annual State Personal Income," Population table (n.d.)
Average Transportation Energy Real Prices = Average Transportation Prices / GDP Deflator	Average price of energy for the transportation sector, in dollars (ESRCD) *Source:* EIA (November 2001)
Disposable Real Income per Capita = Disposable Income per Capita / GDP Deflator	Disposable income per capita *Source:* BEA, *Regional Accounts Data,* "Annual State Personal Income," Per capita disposable personal income table (n.d.)
Employment	Total Employment (010) / Population *Source:* BEA, *Regional Accounts Data,* "Annual State Personal Income," SA25 1980–2001 archive: Total full-time and part-time employment by industry (n.d.)
Real GSP from Local Transit Transportation per Capita	GSP from local and interurban passenger transit, in dollars / GDP deflator / Population *Source:* BEA Web site
Real GSP from Trucking Transportation per Capita	GSP from trucking and warehousing, in dollars / GDP Deflator / Population *Source:* BEA Web site

Data on heating-degree and cooling-degree days were also provided from the EIA. These data are available by census region only, but the heating-degree-days and cooling-degree-days variables by region should be sufficient to identify weather-related variations in energy intensity.

Economic Data

Our source for economic data is the U.S. Department of Commerce Bureau of Economic Analysis, Regional Accounts Data Web site (http://www.bea.doc. gov/bea/regional/data.htm). It contains GSP and employment data disaggregated by energy-consuming sectors and subsectors, disposable income, and the GDP deflator. All dollar-denominated variables that we used in the regressions are transformed into 1999 dollars using the national GDP deflator. The details on the constructed variables are in the following tables.

Demographic Data

Estimates of population and the average number of households and number of individuals per household by state are from the U.S. Census Bureau Web site (http://www.census.gov/). The data used to estimate the variables for the number of households and household size by state start from 1980, which limited the years of our analysis of the residential sector to 1979 through 1999.

B. Regression Analysis Results

In this appendix, we present the results of our analysis of changes in total energy intensity and changes in energy intensity by energy-consuming sector over the period of study (1977–1999).

Total Energy Intensity Regression Results

Our model of annual energy intensity for any given state (among the 48 contiguous states) measures overall energy intensity as the log of total primary energy consumption[1] divided by total GSP. In measuring overall energy intensity, we control for the following variables:

- Log of population per GSP

- Log of average residential energy price

- Log of average transportation energy price

- Log of average industrial energy price

- Log of average commercial energy price

- Log of square footage of commercial floor space/GSP

- Log of percent of GSP from energy-intensive manufacturing[2]

- Log of air transportation GSP per capita

- Heating-degree days

- Cooling-degree days.

Our regression results for total energy intensity are presented in Table B.1. As seen from the table, population per GSP has a large positive effect on total energy intensity. Higher energy prices have a negative effect on total energy intensity, as expected, except for higher commercial energy prices, which have a positive effect. The magnitude of the commercial energy price coefficient is small relative to the energy price coefficients for residential, transportation, and industrial

---

[1]As we stated in Appendix A, primary energy consumption includes both energy consumed by end users and energy losses from the generation and distribution of that energy.

[2]Energy-intensive manufacturing includes manufacturing done in the following industries: paper, glass, primary metals, chemicals, and petroleum.

Table B.1

Total Energy Intensity Regression Variables

Variable	Coefficient	Standard Error	P Value
Population per GSP[a]	0.8508	0.0574	0.0000
Residential Energy Prices[a]	–0.2104	0.0282	0.0000
Transportation Energy Prices[a]	–0.1706	0.0393	0.0000
Industrial Energy Prices[a]	–0.2575	0.0145	0.0000
Commercial Energy Prices[a]	0.0542	0.0181	0.0030
Commercial Floor Space	0.0661	0.0519	0.2030
Energy-Intensive Manufacturing[a]	0.0783	0.0094	0.0000
Air Transportation per GSP[a]	0.0129	0.0052	0.0130
Heating-Degree Days[a]	2.06E-05	6.07E-06	0.0010
Cooling-Degree Days[a]	2.92E-05	1.42E-05	0.0400
Number of Observations		1,104	
R-Squared		0.9854	
Adjusted R-Squared		0.9843	

[a]Significant at the 5% level.
NOTE: All variables except for heating-degree and cooling-degree days are in log form.

energy prices. Also as expected, increases in the share of GSP accounted for by energy-intensive sectors of the economy have a positive effect on energy intensity. Increased numbers of heating-degree and cooling-degree days figure positively in the model but are statistically insignificant.

The adjusted R-squared in this model is very high—more than 0.98. (This is also the case in the sector-specific models described later in this appendix.) Fixed-effect models such as this one tend to have a high R-squared because state and year fixed effects are generally very powerful explanatory variables. That is, much of the variation in energy intensity is fixed across states or over time.

Beyond the issue of bias discussed in Chapter 4, multicollinearity is a potential problem in the regression for overall energy intensity and in the sector-specific regressions discussed later. This is particularly true for residential, commercial, industrial, and transportation energy prices, which no doubt are all influenced by similar factors and therefore vary together over time. Multicollinearity violates no regression assumptions. In practice, though, it can be difficult to obtain precise estimates of the coefficients of correlated variables due to insufficient variation in the data. With high multicollinearity, few coefficients tend to be statistically significant individually, whereas their joint significance is high. In this case, however, our standard errors are reasonable, and most of the variables we include are statistically significant on an individual basis. Also, the coefficient estimates tend to be sensitive to changes in the choice of variables. Our results are robust even with the omission of particular energy price variables. In any case, we are most interested in the joint explanatory power of the included variables because what we care about is the residual energy intensity rather than the effect of any particular included variable. Multicollinearity does not affect estimation of the residual; variation attributable to the independent variables is picked up jointly.

Industrial Energy Intensity Regression Results

The EIA defines the industrial sector as "an energy-consuming sector that consists of all facilities and equipment used for producing, processing, and assembling goods. The industrial sector encompasses the following types of activities: manufacturing; agriculture, forestry, and fisheries; mining; and construction" (EIA, 2000). For our analysis, we use a common measure of industrial energy intensity—energy consumption divided by GSP originating from the industrial sector. The EIA industrial energy consumption data also include fossil fuels used as raw material input for manufactured products. Because nonenergy uses of fuels have little to do with energy efficiency, we made an attempt to exclude nonenergy uses by subtracting fuels that are used solely as feedstock.[3]

We controlled for the following exogenous variables (X) in the industrial energy intensity regression (see Table B.2):

- Sum of heating-degree and cooling-degree days

- Log of industrial energy prices (weighted average)

- Log of percent of petroleum, paper, and metallurgy industries in the industrial sector GSP

- Log of percent of glass and chemical industries in industrial GSP

---

[3]EIA provides energy consumption data by fuel type, not by end use. We are not able to net out all the nonenergy producing uses for fuels because many fuel products can be used as both energy and feedstock. For the purposes of our analysis, we constructed the following energy-consumption variable (also shown in Table A.1):

Industrial primary energy consumption net of feedstocks (Btus) = Total primary energy consumed in the industrial sector (TEICB) less petrochemical feedstocks (naptha less than 401 degrees F [FNICB], other oils equal to or greater than 401 degrees F [FOICB], still gas [FSICB]), asphalt and road oil (ARICB), lubricants (LUICB), special napthas (SNICB), miscellaneous petroleum products (MSICB), and waxes (WXICB).

Table B.2

Industrial Sector Energy Intensity Regression Variables

Variable	Coefficient	Standard Error	P Value
Climate	0.0000277	0.0000177	0.117
Energy Prices[a]	–0.7082609	0.0423190	0.000
Percent of Industrial GSP from Petroleum, Paper, and Metallurgy[a]	0.1268425	0.0200773	0.000
Percent of Industrial GSP from Glass and Chemical	0.0385979	0.0214376	0.072
Percent of Industrial GSP from Food, Textile, and Lumber[a]	0.3253237	0.0274957	0.000
Percent of Industrial GSP from Mining[a]	0.0784011	0.0149293	0.000
Percent of Industrial GSP from Agriculture[a]	0.0943333	0.0238024	0.000
New Capital Expenditures	0.0180824	0.0182403	0.322
Deviation from Equilibrium GSP[a]	0.8347203	0.1135579	0.000
Number of Observations		1,104	
R-Squared		0.940	
Adjusted R-Squared		0.940	

[a]Significant at the 5% level.
NOTE: All variables except for climate are in log form.

- Log of percent of food, textile, and lumber industries in industrial GSP

- Log of percent of mining industry in industrial GSP

- Log of percent of agriculture industry in industrial GSP

- Log of new capital expenditures in the manufacturing subsector divided by GSP in the manufacturing subsector

- Log of percent of deviation from equilibrium industrial GSP.

We used the following equation to estimate the regression:

Industrial energy intensity$_{s,t}$ = a + b_0 Sum of Heating- and Cooling-Degree Days$_{s,t}$ + b_1 Industrial Energy Prices$_{s,t}$ + b_2 Percent of Industrial GSP from Petroleum, Paper, and Metallurgy$_{s,t}$ + b_3 Percent of Industrial GSP from Glass and Chemical$_{s,t}$ + b_4 Percent of Industrial GSP from Food, Textile, and Lumber$_{s,t}$ +b_5 Percent of Industrial GSP from Mining$_{s,t}$ +b_6 Percent of Industrial GSP from Agriculture + b_7 New Capital Expenditures$_{s,t}$ + b_8 Percent Deviation from Equilibrium GSP$_{s,t}$ + State Fixed Effect$_s$ + Time Fixed Effect$_t$

Energy Prices

Higher energy prices are expected to have a negative effect on energy consumption. Higher energy prices should reduce the demand for energy in the industrial sector through more-energy-efficient operations and substituting energy-consuming production methods with methods that use less energy. We use the weighted average of the price of all fuels and find that the effect of prices is significant and has a negative effect on energy intensity.

Structure of Industrial Sector

Structural changes in industrial subsectors that have different energy intensity levels may have a substantial effect on energy use. Using national-level data from the EIA on the energy intensity of industrial subsectors (see Appendix A), we generated five groups of subsectors that are more energy intensive than others to varying degrees. The subsector variables used in this regression are constructed as each subsector's share of the industrial GSP in a log form.

We would expect the effect of these variables to be positive because these industries are more energy intensive than others. Therefore, if their share of the industrial GSP grows, overall industrial sector energy intensity should increase. In the regression, we find a positive effect from an increase in any subsectors' share of the industrial GSP, with only the glass and chemical subsector variables being insignificant.

Capital Turnover

Replacing old capital may decrease energy intensity because energy-efficient technologies develop with time. We define new capital investment in the industrial sector as a percentage of the sector's GSP to approximate the effect of new capital on energy intensity and to control for it. Although this variable also has an effect on energy intensity over later years that diminishes with time, we are not able to account for those changes because our data are limited to the 1977 through 1999 period, and data on the other relevant alternative variable, the age of capital stock, are not available.

Capacity Utilization

Energy consumption per dollar value of output depends on capacity utilization—more energy per output is usually needed when capacity is underutilized because of fixed requirements for energy to run the production process. There is, of course, a limit to this relationship because older equipment may become less efficient if it is used to full capacity. We approximate this factor with a business-cycle measure—percent deviation from equilibrium industrial GSP. We computed equilibrium industrial GSP by smoothing industrial GSP with a backward- and forward-looking moving average.[4] The capacity underutilization proxy is defined as the log of equilibrium industrial GSP divided by the actual GSP. We would expect the sign of the coefficient on this variable to be positive—the larger the underutilization of capacity, the larger the consumption of energy—and it is in fact positive and significant.

Finally, we use climate—the sum of heating-degree and cooling-degree days—to control for changes in energy intensity due to seasonal changes in the weather that may affect the amount of energy needed for heating and air-conditioning. This variable is not significant.

Commercial Energy Intensity Regression Results

Any energy consumption that is not for residential, industrial, or transportation purposes falls into this category, which by convention is referred to as the commercial energy consumption sector.[5] While energy consumed by this sector includes energy used by public offices and for various public purposes, most of the energy use in this sector can be attributed to the production of services. Thus, to measure energy intensity in this sector, we divided energy consumption by the GSP originating from services production (transportation and utilities excluded).

We controlled for the following exogenous variables in the commercial energy intensity regression (see Table B.3):

- Heating-degree days
- Cooling-degree days
- Log of commercial floor space per GSP from services production
- Log of commercial average energy prices
- Log of population per GSP from services production
- Log of commercial sector employment per GSP from services production
- Log of percent of commercial GSP from educational services production

---

[4]A Hodrick-Prescott filter was used to do this computation.

[5]The commercial sector is defined in the EIA database as "an energy-consuming sector that consists of the service-providing facilities and the equipment of businesses; federal, state, and local governments; and other private and public organizations ... [and] institutional living headquarters."

Table B.3

Commercial Sector Energy Intensity Regression Variables

Variable	Coefficient	Standard Error	P Value
Heating-Degree Days[a]	0.0000741	0.0000136	0.000
Cooling-Degree Days[a]	0.0000633	0.0000315	0.045
Floor Space per GSP from Services	–0.1143808	0.1152337	0.321
Energy Prices[a]	–0.2044511	0.0368456	0.000
Population per GSP from Services	0.1540582	0.1403543	0.273
Employment per GSP from Services[a]	0.9142759	0.1171089	0.000
Commercial GSP from Education	0.0532051	0.0450773	0.238
Commercial GSP from Retail Trade[a]	–0.4582944	0.0869897	0.000
Commercial GSP from F.I.R.E. and Legal[a]	0.1943485	0.0904856	0.032
Commercial GSP from Health[a]	0.2080429	0.0628284	0.001
Number of Observations		1,104	
R-Squared		0.891	
Adjusted R-Squared		0.882	

[a]Significant at the 5% level.
NOTE: All variables except for heating-degree days and cooling-degree days are in log form.

- Log of percent of commercial GSP from retail trade

- Log of percent of commercial GSP from F.I.R.E. and legal services production

- Log of percent of commercial GSP from health industry production.

We used the following equation to estimate the regression:

Commercial Energy Intensity$_{s,t}$ = a + b_0 Heating-Degree Days$_{s,t}$ +b_1 Cooling-Degree Days$_{s,t}$ + b_2 Commercial Floor Space$_{s,t}$ + b_3 Commercial Energy Prices$_{s,t}$ + b_4 Population/Commercial GSP$_{s,t}$ + b_5 Commercial Sector Employment$_{s,t}$ + b_6 Percent of Commercial GSP from Educational Services (reserve)$_{s,t}$ + b_7 Percent of Commercial GSP from Retail Trade$_{s,t}$ + b_8 Percent of Commercial GSP from F.I.R.E. and Legal$_{s,t}$ + b_9 Percent of Commercial GSP from Health$_{s,t}$+ State Fixed Effect$_s$ + Time Fixed Effect$_t$

Energy Prices

Energy prices are expected to have a negative effect on energy consumption because rising energy prices may stimulate energy conservation and efficiency measures in the commercial sector. We use a weighted average of the prices of all fuels and find that the effect of rising energy prices on energy intensity is significant and negative.

Commercial Floor Space

Heating, lighting, and air-conditioning consume a major portion of the energy used by this sector. The consumption of energy for these purposes depends on the square footage of floor space in buildings, which is why commercial floor space is included in the regression. We would expect increasing square footage of floor space to have a positive effect on energy intensity; however, we found in the regression that floor space per GSP in the commercial sector is insignificant. It may be the case that square footage of floor space would be a significant variable if we were able to disaggregate the regression according to building type.

Employment in the Commercial Sector and Population

It is possible that the more customers the commercial sector must serve, and the more employees working in the sector, the more energy is required per GSP. To control for these effects, we use population and employment variables, both divided by the GSP from services. Of the two variables, only employment per GSP is significant, and it is positive, an indication that the greater the employment per dollar of economic growth, the more energy intensive a state's commercial sector is. The insignificance of population and floor space variables may be related to the multicollinearity in these variables and in employment in the commercial sector.

Structure of the Commercial Sector

Structural changes in the commercial sector among more-energy-intensive and less-energy-intensive subsectors may have a substantial effect on energy use. Using the available literature and data,[6] we selected four subsectors that may have different energy per GSP ratios: education, retail trade, F.I.R.E and legal services, and health services. Only the retail trade and health sectors are significant. Retail trade is negative (the greater the proportion of the retail trade

---

[6]The literature on energy intensity (i.e., EIA, 1995) identifies building types, such as offices, retail establishments, education facilities, hospitals, and other types of buildings, with varying energy intensity. Because panel data on building types are unavailable, we use the proportion of GSP from the various types of services, which correspond to the various buildings types, to create the variables on the subsectors.

subsector, the lower the energy intensity), and health is positive (the greater the proportion of the health subsector, the higher the energy intensity). The latter makes sense because health services tend to be more energy intensive than other services.

We also use heating-degree and cooling-degree days to control for changes in energy intensity due to seasonal weather changes that may affect the energy required for heating and air-conditioning in the sector.

Residential Energy Intensity Regression Results

Energy intensity in the residential sector is usually measured as energy consumption per capita, per household, or per square foot of the residential building space. For our regression model, we use energy consumption per capita as the dependent variable in the regression. It is a reasonable measure because demand for all end uses of energy, including heating, air-conditioning, water heating, and powering appliances, directly or indirectly (i.e., through the size of the dwelling space) depends on the number of people using the energy.

However, the residential demand for energy depends on a number of factors other than population. We used the following variables in the regression analysis for residential energy intensity (see Table B.4). All the variables are significant.

- Heating-degree days
- Cooling-degree days
- Log of residential electricity prices
- Log of residential natural gas prices
- Log of average household size
- Log of real disposable income per capita
- Log of employment per capita.

We used the following equation to estimate the regression:

Residential Energy Intensity$_{s,t}$ = a + b_0 Heating-Degree Days$_{s,t}$ + b_1 Cooling-Degree Days$_{s,t}$ + b_2 Residential Electricity Prices$_{s,t}$ + b_3 Residential Natural Gas Prices$_{s,t}$ + b_4 Disposable Income per Capita$_{s,t}$ + b_5 Employment per Capita$_{s,t}$ + b_6 Average Household Size$_{s,t}$ + State Fixed Effect$_s$ + Time Fixed Effect$_t$

Table B.4

Residential Sector Energy Intensity Regression Variables

Variable	Coefficient	Standard Error	P Value
Heating-Degree Days[a]	0.0000742	5.54e-06	0.000
Cooling-Degree Days[a]	0.0000650	0.0000126	0.000
Electricity Prices[a]	–0.1314553	0.0188106	0.000
Natural Gas Prices[a]	0.0681121	0.0157596	0.000
Disposable Income per Capita[a]	0.3952117	0.0419841	0.000
Employment per Capita[a]	–0.4340120	0.0524521	0.000
Household Size[a]	1.8050550	0.1148474	0.000
Number of Observations		960	
R-Squared		0.924	
Adjusted R-Squared		0.918	

[a]Significant at the 5% level.

NOTE: All variables except for heating-degree days and cooling-degree days are in log form.

Energy Prices

Demand for energy depends on its price. Increases in the price of energy drive people to reduce their energy consumption. The primary energy sources in the residential sector are electricity and natural gas, plus oil to a lesser extent for heating. If the comparative prices of different fuels change, people may substitute one fuel for another (i.e., if the price of natural gas rises, consumers can switch to electricity for heating). We take this effect into account because primary energy consumption (the dependent variable) is sensitive to changes in the mix of fuels being consumed—a larger share of electricity means greater energy losses in generation and transmission, which may increase primary energy consumption even if consumers use the same amount of energy on site.

We include the prices of two major fuels, electricity and natural gas, to produce the regression. Higher electricity prices have a negative effect on energy intensity, due to both reduced energy use and consumers switching to alternative fuels when price goes up. A priori, the effect of the price of natural gas on energy intensity is ambiguous: A higher price for natural gas may reduce total energy used from natural gas, but if its relative price increases consistently over time, people may switch to electricity, which on a "source energy" basis is less efficient than natural gas. From the regression analysis, we can see that natural gas has positive price elasticity—that is, as the price of natural gas goes up, energy intensity goes up due to the substitution of electricity for gas.

Household Size

Household size affects how much energy is needed per person due to economies of scale of heating, air-conditioning, cooking, lighting, and other uses of energy. Also, household size correlates with the floor space in a dwelling per person, an important factor we cannot explicitly account for.[7] We expected the effect of household size on energy intensity to be negative—the larger the household, the less energy is needed per person. The regression in fact shows this to be the case.[8]

Disposable Income

Disposable income affects energy consumption in several ways. First, increases in income allow people to buy more energy-consuming appliances, but it also enables them to use more energy for all purposes because energy expenses become a smaller part of their income. Income also correlates with residential living space per person because higher incomes make it possible for people to live in larger houses, which require more energy for heating and air-conditioning. However, higher income may also decrease energy consumption in the residential sector because it enables homeowners to buy new and more-energy-efficient devices to replace older and less-energy-efficient ones. Higher income also enables families to shift some household activities, such as laundry and cooking, to the commercial sector, which reduces energy use in the residential sector. Although increased income per capita affects energy consumption in different ways, on average in the regression the effect is positive.

Time People Spend at Home

Another factor that may affect residential energy intensity is the amount of time people spend at home—the less time spent at home, the lower the household energy use. As a proxy for this factor and for possibly capturing other effects, we use employment per capita. It is possible that higher employment results in people spending more time at work than in the home, and may also account for substitution of some energy-consuming services, such as child care, cooking, and laundry, to the commercial sector. In our regression analysis, employment has a negative effect on energy consumption.

---

[7]Good-quality data on residential floor space by state are not available.

[8]The data for this variable are available by state starting from only 1979, which, as we stated earlier in this report, limits the time period we cover in the analysis of the residential sector to 1979–1999.

Climate and Weather

Energy demand for heating and air-conditioning depends on a state's climate and weather. While we expect climate differences among states to be picked up by the state's fixed effects in the regression, we have to also account for fluctuations in weather from year to year, the patterns of which may vary across states. We use heating-degree and cooling-degree day[9] variables to capture this effect. Both are expected to have a positive effect on energy consumption. Heating and cooling variables are assumed to have a log-linear relationship with energy intensity, while all other variables are assumed to have a log-log relationship.[10]

Transportation Energy Intensity Regression Results

The transportation sector encompasses both private and public passenger transportation as well as freight transportation. We have to deviate from traditional measures of energy intensity in this sector because we do not have data on the denominator variables—vehicle miles, passenger miles, or ton miles traveled—and because there are no separate data on passenger transportation and freight transportation energy consumption. Instead, we use energy consumption per person (because a large portion of energy is consumed by passenger transportation), and population in some ways controls for the size of a state. In this analysis, we subtract the energy used for air transport because it is not clear how much air transport relates to individual state actions. Also, air transport varies widely and significantly influences energy intensity.

We controlled for the following exogenous variables in the regression on transportation energy intensity (see Table B.5):

- Log of transportation energy prices (weighted average)
- Log of disposable income per capita
- Log of employment per capita
- Log of local passenger transit GSP per capita
- Log of trucking GSP per capita

---

[9]These variables are not available by state for the study period; instead, they are by geographical regions that include a group of states.

[10]All the variables other than heating-degree days and cooling-degree days are transformed into log form.

'Table B.5

Transportation Sector Energy Intensity Regression Variables

Variable	Coefficient	Standard Error	P Value
Average Price of Energy [a]	−0.333	0.043	0.000
Disposable Income per Capita[a]	0.127	0.051	0.014
Employment per Capita[a]	0.878	0.061	0.000
Public Transit	−0.012	0.011	0.269
Portion of GSP from Trucking	0.026	0.018	0.152
Number of Observations		1104	
R-Squared		0.955	
Adjusted R-Squared		0.9505	

[a]Significant at the 5% level.
NOTE: All variables are in log form.

We used the following equation to estimate the regression:

Transportation Energy Intensity$_{s,t}$ = a + b_0 Average Transportation Energy Price$_{s,t}$ + b_1 Disposable Income per Capita$_{s,t}$ + b_2 Employment per Capita$_{s,t}$ + b_3 Local Passenger Transit GSP per Capita$_{s,t}$ + b_4 Trucking GSP per Capita$_{s,t}$ + b_4 Air Transportation GSP per Capita$_{s,t}$ + State Fixed Effect$_s$ + Time Fixed Effect$_t$

Because most of the fuels consumed in transportation sector are based on petroleum, and because it is not easy to substitute fuels in a vehicle, we use a weighted average of all fuel prices for the transportation sector analysis. We expect the coefficient of the average-price-of-energy variable to have a negative sign because energy consumption goes down when the price of energy increases. This variable is significant in the regression.

Disposable income affects vehicle ownership rates and the affordability of traveling. We would expect this variable to have a positive coefficient, which it in fact does. This variable is significant.

Employment increases the number of people who commute to work, which may affect vehicle miles traveled and modes of passenger transport. This variable is positive and significant in the regression.

Public transit has an ambiguous effect on energy consumption. Public transit is less energy intensive per person than individual-vehicle commuting. Therefore, less energy is consumed if mass transportation substitutes for inefficient private-vehicle transportation, and if that mass transit is well used, because an underused public transportation system could increase energy intensity. In the regression, this variable is insignificant.

We also control for a large portion of the transportation sector's GSP from freight transportation—the portion of the GSP from trucking. The larger the share of the freight transportation GSP from trucking, the more energy per capita is consumed by the transportation sector; however, this variable is not significant in the regression.

Overall, our analysis of the transportation sector's energy intensity by state is likely to suffer from measurement errors. A large share of all transportation is interstate, and it is difficult to distribute variables related to interstate transportation among all states.

C. Methodology for Calculating the What-Ifs in Chapter 8

In Chapter 8, we estimated what might happen to energy intensity nationwide by 2020 if all states had the same changes in energy intensity as the five states with the largest unexplained reductions in energy intensity since 1988. We also estimated what might happen if all states had the same energy intensity changes as the five states that had unexplained changes in energy intensity that resulted in lower rates of reduction in energy intensity than would have been expected. The two estimations supplied the upper and lower bounds for our predictions on nationwide reductions in energy intensity. In addition, we performed the total calculation in two ways—using a simple extrapolation and using a prediction method.

Extrapolation of Change in Overall Energy Intensity

From 1988 to 1999, the average annual decrease in energy intensity was around 1.62 percent across the 48 contiguous states. Of this decrease, 0.87 percent is attributed to changes in the factors that we control for in our regression model: energy prices, population, weather (heating-degree and cooling-degree days), percentage of GDP originating from energy-intensive industries, commercial floor space, and air transportation. The rest of the decrease (0.74 percent) is due to other factors that we did not account for in the model and that were the same for all the states (e.g., national policies, technology advances).

If the factors we just listed follow their historic patterns, energy intensity would continue to decrease at a rate of 1.62 percent per year on average across the 48 contiguous states. However, some states performed better than others regardless of the aforementioned factors. If we assume that most of the change in the states' energy intensity was the result of policies that these states have implemented, and if all states in the future replicate the performance of best-performing states, then we can estimate a different future energy intensity. The additional average decrease in energy intensity of the five top-ranked states over the 1988–1999 period, beyond the 1.62 percent average decrease across all states, is around 0.78 percent.

Thus, if all states were to follow the actions of the top five performing states, energy intensity would decrease by 2.4 percent per year on average across the 48 states. However, if every state had the same unexplained changes as the five states with the largest increase in energy intensity (1.07 percent on average), energy intensity would decrease only by 0.55 percent annually.

Table C.1 demonstrates how various factors affected changes in energy intensity (on average across the 48 states). The effect of each variable is calculated as a percentage change in the variable over the 1988–1999 period multiplied by its estimated coefficient if the variable is logged, or as an absolute change in the variable multiplied by its coefficient if the variable is not logged (applies to the heating-degree-days and cooling-degree-days variables only).

Extrapolation of Change in Sector-Level Energy Intensity

We extrapolated sector-level energy intensity based on the results of our analysis for the period 1988–1999, the results of which we discuss next.[1]

Residential Sector Energy Intensity

The average annual decrease in residential sector energy intensity for this period was 0.05 percent across the 48 states. The variables we accounted for contributed 0.73 percent of this change, and the common and fixed effects contributed –0.78 percent. If every state experienced reductions in energy intensity at the same average rate as the five best-performing states (ranked by the change in residuals), energy intensity would change by –0.65 percent annually, summing to a –0.70 percent change in residential sector energy intensity nationwide per year. Alternatively, if every state experienced the same average trend as the five states with the largest increases in energy intensity, residential energy intensity would increase 0.6 percent per year on average.

Commercial Sector Energy Intensity

In the commercial sector, the average annual change in energy intensity was –1.9 percent over 1988–1999, of which –1.0 percent was due to changes in variables, and –0.9 percent was due to changes in common and fixed effects. Replicating the

---

[1]We omitted discussion of the transportation sector in this appendix because of difficulties in interpreting transportation sector data (see Chapter 6).

Table C.1

Predicted Average Annual Changes in Energy Intensity Due to Various Factors, 1988–1999, Using Extrapolation Method

Variable	Coefficient	Average Annual Change in Variable	Effect of Change in Variable on Energy Intensity
Commercial Floor Space per GSP	0.0661	–1.46%	–0.10%
Heating-Degree Days	2.06E-05	–13.37	–0.03%
Cooling-Degree Days	2.92E-05	1.13	0.00%
Population per GSP	0.8508	–2.15%	–1.83%
Share of Air Transportation in GSP	0.0129	6.74%	0.09%
Share of Energy-Intensive Manufacturing in GSP	0.0783	–0.52%	–0.04%
Transportation Energy Prices	–0.1706	–0.71%	0.12%
Residential Energy Prices	–0.2104	–1.04%	0.22%
Commercial Energy Prices	0.0542	–1.26%	–0.07%
Industrial Energy Prices	–0.2575	–2.93%	0.76%
Total Change Due to Variables			–0.74%

average residuals trend of the five best-performing states in the other 43 states would result in an energy intensity reduction of 1.27 percent, thereby producing a –3.17 percent change in commercial sector energy intensity nationwide. Replicating the trend in the states with the largest increase or smallest decreases would reduce energy intensity by 0.54 percent annually.

Industrial Sector Energy Intensity

The industrial sector historically has had a –0.23 percent change in energy intensity per year. A 1.36 percent change was due to changes in variables and a –1.59 percent change was due to time effects. Replicating the trend in residuals of the five best-performing states in the other states would change industrial energy intensity by –2.98 percent, which totals to a –3.21 percent annual change in industrial sector energy intensity across the country. However, if every state experienced the trend in residuals of the five states with the largest increases in energy intensity, average annual industrial energy intensity would increase by 2.55 percent.

Prediction of Change in Overall Energy Intensity

The estimated coefficients from our regression analysis can be used to forecast future changes in energy intensity given the projections or forecasts of exogenous variables.[2] Our model forecasts an annual energy intensity decrease of 1.5 percent per year under these assumptions.

By multiplying the predicted average annual change[3] in an independent variable by the corresponding coefficient from our regression, we obtain the percentage change in energy intensity due to that variable. We use the EIA's reference case forecast for the year 2020 for the average annual change in GDP, energy prices, and commercial floor space, and we use U.S. Census Bureau predictions of population growth (http://www.census.gov/). We extrapolate the historic changes (over the 1988–1999 period) in the share of energy-intensive manufacturing, the share of air transportation, and climate change (heating-degree and cooling-degree days). These assumptions yield the results shown in Table C.2.

The forecasted variables for the 1988–1999 period result in much larger improvements in energy intensity than does the extrapolation from the

Table C.2

Predicted Average Annual Changes in Energy Intensity Due to Various Factors, 1988–1999, Using Prediction Method

Variable	Coefficient	Average Annual Change in the Variable	Effect of Change in the Variable on Energy Intensity
Commercial Floor Space per GSP	0.0661	−1.30%	−0.09%
Heating-Degree Days	2.06E-05	0	0.00%
Cooling-Degree Days	2.92E-05	0	0.00%
Population per GSP	0.8508	−2.07%	−1.76%
Share of Air Transportation in GSP	0.0129	0.05%	0.00%
Share of Energy-Intensive Manufacturing in GSP	0.0783	−1.33%	−0.10%
Transportation Energy Prices	−0.1706	−0.40%	0.07%
Residential Energy Prices	−0.2104	−0.10%	0.02%
Commercial Energy Prices	0.0542	−0.20%	−0.01%
Industrial Energy Prices	−0.2575	−0.30%	0.08%
Change Due to All Variables			−1.79%
Change Due to Time Effects			−0.74%
Total Change			−2.53%

---

[2] The EIA's projection of energy prices and economic indicators for each year can be found at the EIA's Annual Energy Outlook site at www.eia.doe.gov/oiaf/aeo/index.html.

[3] For all the variables, except for heating-degree days and cooling-degree days, the changes are expressed as percentages because the variables are logged.

1988–1999 period: a –1.79 percent change versus a 0.87 percent change, respectively. The total average annual change in energy intensity is forecasted to be –2.53 percent if one were to apply the 1988–1999 time-effects trend.

This forecast can show further improvements in energy intensity if one were to also assume that all states experienced the same average residual energy intensity reduction of the five best-performing states. The average decrease in energy intensity in 1988–1999 for the top five states, over and above the average of all 48 states, is approximately 0.78 percent. If every state followed the average pattern of the top-performing states, energy intensity nationwide could be decreased by 3.31 percent (the total average annual change of –2.53 percent plus the additional 0.78 average reduction of the top states). Alternatively, if every state exhibited the same average pattern as the states with the largest increases in energy intensity, energy intensity would decrease by only 1.46 percent annually.

D. Detailed Results of Energy Intensity Analysis

Tables D.1 through D.3 list detailed data on the changes in energy intensity in each of the 48 contiguous states over the entire study period 1977–1999 and over the subperiods 1977–1988 and 1989–1999. The tables also rank the states according to the amount of change in residual energy intensity. The results are presented by individual energy-consuming sector and by all four sectors collectively (total aggregate).

The following list defines the column headlines in the tables:

- Raw Energy Intensity Average % Change = Energy intensity average percent change over the time period (average intensity percent change equals the residual plus the factor effect plus the time effect).

- Residual Average % Change = Average percent change in energy intensity due to the residual over the time period.

- Variate Average % Percent Change = Average percent change in energy intensity due to the factors measured in the regression analyses.

- Residual Ranking = How the state ranks in its change in residual energy intensity. The states are ranked in order from 1 to 48, with the state ranked 1 having the greatest reduction in residual energy intensity.

- Movement = How much the residual ranking moved from the Raw Energy Intensity Average % Change. For example, a residual ranking of 15 and a movement of –5 means that the state ranked 10th in the amount of actual energy intensity changes.

Table D.1A

Energy Intensity Analysis Data for the Entire Study Period 1977–1999: Industrial, Commercial, and Residential Sectors

State	Industrial Sector					Commercial Sector					Residential Sector				
	Raw Energy Intensity Average % Change	Residual Average % Change	Variate Average % Change	Residual Ranking	Move-ment	Raw Energy Intensity Average % Change	Residual Average % Change	Variate Average % Change	Residual Ranking	Move-ment	Raw Energy Intensity Average % Change	Residual Average % Change	Variate Average % Change	Residual Ranking	Move-ment
Alabama	-0.92%	-0.58%	0.58%	13	11	-0.91%	1.23%	-1.05%	46	-3	0.56%	0.24%	1.40%	37	9
Arizona	-4.59%	-1.55%	-2.11%	6	-5	-2.84%	-1.04%	-0.71%	4	2	-0.10%	0.14%	0.85%	33	-3
Arkansas	0.35%	0.79%	0.48%	38	4	-2.68%	-0.52%	-1.06%	11	-4	-0.43%	-0.40%	1.06%	5	8
California	-1.01%	0.15%	-0.25%	28	-7	-3.27%	-1.14%	-1.04%	3	1	-1.14%	-0.05%	0.00%	21	-19
Colorado	-2.53%	-0.09%	-1.52%	23	-14	-2.06%	0.16%	-1.13%	31	-9	-0.12%	0.06%	0.91%	29	-1
Connecticut	-2.75%	-1.32%	-0.50%	8	-1	-2.66%	0.08%	-1.64%	28	-20	-0.04%	-0.11%	1.16%	17	16
Delaware	-0.07%	0.52%	0.33%	31	8	-5.00%	0.37%	-4.28%	37	-36	0.21%	0.04%	1.25%	28	9
Florida	-1.99%	-0.50%	-0.57%	15	-4	-1.74%	0.29%	-0.94%	35	-1	0.30%	0.66%	0.73%	48	-7
Georgia	-0.90%	-0.40%	0.42%	17	8	-2.41%	-0.12%	-1.19%	21	-7	0.26%	0.30%	1.05%	41	-3
Idaho	-1.43%	0.94%	-1.46%	41	-26	-2.13%	-0.98%	-0.06%	6	12	-0.15%	0.49%	0.45%	46	-20
Illinois	-0.99%	0.62%	-0.69%	33	-11	-3.05%	-0.99%	-0.96%	5	0	-0.57%	0.07%	0.45%	30	-22
Indiana	-1.65%	-0.26%	-0.47%	20	-7	-1.92%	-0.28%	-0.54%	14	16	-0.23%	0.09%	0.77%	31	-8
Iowa	1.25%	0.73%	1.44%	36	10	-1.99%	-0.44%	-0.46%	12	14	-0.50%	0.01%	0.58%	25	-16
Kansas	-1.13%	0.80%	-1.01%	39	-20	-1.88%	0.33%	-1.11%	36	-5	-0.30%	0.25%	0.54%	38	-17
Kentucky	-0.66%	-0.06%	0.32%	25	3	-2.09%	0.09%	-1.09%	29	-10	0.49%	0.35%	1.23%	43	1
Louisiana	-0.55%	-0.27%	0.64%	19	14	-2.51%	-0.60%	-0.82%	8	1	0.34%	0.32%	1.11%	42	0
Maine	1.22%	1.92%	0.22%	45	0	-1.97%	0.06%	-0.94%	27	0	0.17%	0.19%	1.07%	36	0
Maryland	-3.40%	-2.71%	0.23%	1	1	-0.56%	0.99%	-0.45%	44	1	0.14%	0.04%	1.19%	27	7
Massachusetts	-0.62%	-0.08%	0.38%	24	8	-4.57%	-1.61%	-1.86%	1	1	-0.35%	-0.61%	1.35%	2	17
Michigan	-0.64%	-0.03%	0.31%	26	3	-0.93%	0.89%	-0.73%	41	1	-0.49%	-0.16%	0.76%	13	-3
Minnesota	-0.50%	1.10%	-0.68%	43	-7	-2.47%	-0.26%	-1.12%	15	-4	-0.36%	-0.17%	0.90%	12	6
Mississippi	0.33%	0.61%	0.64%	32	9	-0.97%	0.94%	-0.82%	43	-2	0.58%	0.37%	1.31%	44	3
Missouri	-1.59%	-0.69%	0.02%	12	2	-2.07%	-0.08%	-0.90%	22	-2	-0.40%	-0.06%	0.75%	20	-3
Montana	0.91%	2.38%	-0.55%	48	-4	-2.00%	-0.83%	-0.07%	7	18	-0.68%	-0.24%	0.65%	8	-3
Nebraska	-1.35%	0.11%	-0.54%	27	-11	-2.47%	-0.57%	-0.81%	10	3	-0.30%	0.10%	0.68%	32	-12
Nevada	-0.63%	2.28%	-1.98%	47	-17	-3.28%	-1.41%	-0.78%	2	1	-1.03%	-0.35%	0.41%	6	-3

Table D.1A—Continued

State	Industrial Sector					Commercial Sector					Residential Sector				
	Raw Energy Intensity Average % Change	Residual Average % Change	Variate Average % Change	Residual Ranking	Move-ment	Raw Energy Intensity Average % Change	Residual Average % Change	Variate Average % Change	Residual Ranking	Move-ment	Raw Energy Intensity Average % Change	Residual Average % Change	Variate Average % Change	Residual Ranking	Move-ment
New Hampshire	-2.80%	-0.83%	-1.05%	11	-5	-0.80%	1.95%	-1.65%	48	-4	-0.13%	-0.10%	1.05%	19	8
New Jersey	-0.63%	-0.84%	1.14%	9	22	-2.49%	-0.15%	-1.25%	20	-10	-0.41%	-0.20%	0.88%	9	7
New Mexico	-3.04%	-0.44%	-1.69%	16	-12	-1.58%	-0.18%	-0.31%	19	17	-0.06%	-0.02%	1.05%	23	9
New York	-0.98%	-0.52%	0.47%	14	9	-2.34%	-0.26%	-0.99%	16	-1	-0.10%	0.39%	0.59%	45	-16
North Carolina	-1.94%	-0.84%	-0.18%	10	2	-1.42%	0.49%	-0.81%	40	-2	0.17%	-0.16%	1.42%	14	21
North Dakota	4.85%	2.16%	3.61%	46	2	-0.13%	1.29%	-0.32%	47	0	0.38%	0.29%	1.18%	39	4
Ohio	-1.26%	-0.27%	-0.07%	18	-1	-1.78%	0.22%	-0.90%	33	0	-0.46%	-0.11%	0.74%	18	-6
Oklahoma	-0.72%	-0.23%	0.42%	21	6	-1.41%	-0.01%	-0.30%	26	13	-0.15%	0.30%	0.64%	40	-15
Oregon	-2.96%	0.75%	-2.79%	37	-32	-2.07%	-0.58%	-0.40%	9	12	-0.41%	0.15%	0.52%	34	-19
Pennsylvania	-2.47%	-1.50%	-0.05%	7	3	-1.94%	-0.24%	-0.61%	17	12	-0.61%	-0.56%	1.04%	3	4
Rhode Island	1.61%	0.66%	1.87%	35	12	-2.47%	-0.29%	-1.08%	13	-1	-0.06%	-0.20%	1.22%	10	21
South Carolina	-0.54%	0.93%	-0.55%	40	-6	-2.34%	-0.18%	-1.07%	18	-2	0.71%	0.02%	1.78%	26	22
South Dakota	-1.21%	-1.92%	1.63%	2	16	-2.01%	-0.07%	-0.84%	23	1	-0.42%	-0.13%	0.80%	15	-1
Tennessee	-2.72%	-1.83%	0.04%	4	4	-1.35%	0.92%	-1.18%	42	-2	-0.24%	-0.27%	1.11%	7	15
Texas	-0.43%	-0.22%	0.71%	22	15	-2.19%	-0.02%	-1.08%	25	-8	-0.23%	0.18%	0.68%	35	-11
Utah	-3.18%	-1.84%	-0.42%	3	0	-1.80%	-0.07%	-0.63%	24	8	-1.20%	-0.76%	0.65%	1	0
Vermont	-0.74%	0.63%	-0.45%	34	-8	-2.03%	0.25%	-1.19%	34	-11	-0.64%	-0.48%	0.93%	4	2
Virginia	0.05%	0.42%	0.55%	29	11	-1.56%	0.44%	-0.91%	39	-2	0.29%	-0.05%	1.43%	22	17
Washington	-1.10%	0.98%	-1.16%	42	-22	-1.96%	0.17%	-1.04%	32	-4	-0.72%	-0.02%	0.39%	24	-20
West Virginia	-0.50%	-1.56%	1.98%	5	30	-0.18%	0.41%	0.50%	38	8	0.30%	-0.13%	1.52%	16	24
Wisconsin	-0.39%	0.45%	0.08%	30	8	-1.64%	0.15%	-0.69%	30	5	-0.48%	-0.19%	0.80%	11	0
Wyoming	0.64%	1.49%	0.08%	44	-1	0.50%	1.17%	0.42%	45	3	0.50%	0.50%	1.08%	47	-2
Statewide Average	-0.96%		-0.05%			-1.99%		-0.89%			-0.17%		0.92%		

Table D.1B

Energy Intensity Analysis Data for the Entire Study Period 1977–1999: Transportation Sector and Total Aggregate

State	Transportation Sector					Total Aggregate Energy Intensity				
	Raw Energy Intensity Average % Change	Residual Average % Change	Variate Average % Change	Residual Ranking	Move-ment	Raw Energy Intensity Average % Change	Residual Average % Change	Variate Average % Change	Residual Ranking	Move-ment
Alabama	-1.05%	-1.29%	1.50%	1	0	-1.91%	0.06%	-1.49%	29	3
Arizona	-0.43%	-0.59%	1.42%	5	1	-3.07%	-0.57%	-2.02%	2	3
Arkansas	0.34%	-0.18%	1.77%	14	16	-1.48%	0.43%	-1.43%	42	-2
California	-0.78%	-0.52%	0.99%	7	-3	-2.54%	-0.41%	-1.64%	8	4
Colorado	-0.23%	-0.52%	1.54%	6	3	-2.87%	-0.02%	-2.37%	26	-19
Connecticut	0.24%	0.21%	1.28%	36	-15	-3.18%	0.12%	-2.82%	30	-26
Delaware	0.53%	0.25%	1.54%	37	-2	-3.32%	-0.44%	-2.40%	5	-2
Florida	-0.04%	-0.28%	1.50%	11	0	-2.30%	-0.29%	-1.53%	11	10
Georgia	0.60%	0.04%	1.81%	25	11	-2.35%	0.23%	-2.10%	38	-19
Idaho	0.09%	0.12%	1.22%	31	-16	-1.86%	-0.12%	-1.26%	22	12
Illinois	0.13%	0.06%	1.33%	27	-10	-2.61%	-0.43%	-1.70%	6	5
Indiana	0.79%	0.31%	1.73%	39	3	-1.92%	-0.34%	-1.09%	9	22
Iowa	0.30%	-0.13%	1.69%	17	7	-0.93%	0.49%	-0.94%	44	1
Kansas	-0.54%	-0.83%	1.55%	3	2	-2.16%	0.14%	-1.82%	34	-12
Kentucky	0.89%	0.42%	1.73%	44	0	-1.50%	-0.05%	-0.97%	25	14
Louisiana	-0.03%	-0.39%	1.62%	9	3	-1.54%	-0.22%	-0.83%	13	25
Maine	0.44%	0.13%	1.57%	32	1	-1.72%	0.55%	-1.79%	45	-9
Maryland	0.06%	-0.18%	1.50%	13	1	-2.53%	-0.12%	-1.93%	21	-8
Massachusetts	0.33%	-0.02%	1.60%	22	6	-3.53%	-0.41%	-2.64%	7	-6
Michigan	0.38%	-0.06%	1.70%	18	14	-1.39%	-0.19%	-0.71%	16	26
Minnesota	0.71%	0.19%	1.78%	35	5	-1.97%	0.56%	-2.05%	46	-16
Mississippi	1.15%	0.73%	1.67%	45	1	-0.74%	0.76%	-1.02%	47	-1
Missouri	0.71%	0.35%	1.62%	41	-2	-1.80%	0.26%	-1.57%	39	-4
Montana	0.33%	0.27%	1.31%	38	-9	-1.01%	0.14%	-0.67%	33	11
Nebraska	0.31%	-0.15%	1.72%	15	12	-2.12%	-0.13%	-1.51%	19	5
Nevada	-0.95%	-0.41%	0.72%	8	-5	-2.30%	-0.29%	-1.53%	12	8

Table D.1B—Continued

State	Transportation Sector					Total Aggregate Energy Intensity				
	Raw Energy Intensity Average % Change	Residual Average % Change	Variate Average % Change	Residual Ranking	Move-ment	Raw Energy Intensity Average % Change	Residual Average % Change	Variate Average % Change	Residual Ranking	Move-ment
New Hampshire	0.81%	0.37%	1.70%	42	1	-3.40%	0.13%	-3.04%	32	-30
New Jersey	0.52%	0.07%	1.71%	28	6	-2.36%	0.01%	-1.88%	27	-9
New Mexico	-0.05%	0.00%	1.20%	23	-13	-2.15%	-0.13%	-1.54%	18	5
New York	0.01%	0.05%	1.21%	26	-13	-2.73%	-0.22%	-2.02%	14	-5
North Carolina	0.26%	-0.05%	1.57%	20	2	-2.45%	-0.12%	-1.85%	23	-8
North Dakota	1.35%	0.88%	1.73%	46	1	0.99%	1.45%	0.02%	48	0
Ohio	0.31%	0.01%	1.55%	24	1	-2.05%	0.02%	-1.58%	28	0
Oklahoma	0.28%	-0.03%	1.56%	21	2	-1.41%	-0.12%	-0.80%	20	21
Oregon	-0.38%	-0.26%	1.13%	12	-5	-2.39%	-0.17%	-1.74%	17	0
Pennsylvania	0.31%	0.15%	1.42%	33	-7	-2.74%	-0.56%	-1.70%	4	4
Rhode Island	0.13%	0.33%	1.06%	40	-22	-2.10%	0.17%	-1.78%	36	-9
South Carolina	0.69%	0.39%	1.55%	43	-5	-1.88%	0.43%	-1.83%	43	-10
South Dakota	0.77%	0.19%	1.84%	34	7	-2.00%	-0.07%	-1.45%	24	5
Tennessee	0.17%	-0.31%	1.74%	10	9	-2.88%	-0.56%	-1.83%	3	3
Texas	-1.02%	-1.10%	1.33%	2	0	-2.10%	-0.33%	-1.29%	10	16
Utah	-0.35%	-0.72%	1.63%	4	4	-2.68%	-0.70%	-1.49%	1	9
Vermont	0.62%	0.08%	1.80%	30	7	-2.48%	0.42%	-2.41%	41	-27
Virginia	0.20%	-0.13%	1.59%	16	4	-2.11%	0.16%	-1.79%	35	-10
Washington	0.11%	-0.06%	1.42%	19	-3	-2.42%	0.12%	-2.05%	31	-15
West Virginia	1.10%	0.96%	1.40%	47	-2	-1.25%	-0.21%	-0.55%	15	28
Wisconsin	0.36%	0.07%	1.54%	29	2	-1.69%	0.22%	-1.42%	37	0
Wyoming	1.37%	1.58%	1.04%	48	0	-0.04%	0.36%	0.08%	40	7
Statewide Average	0.25%		1.50%			-2.06%		-1.58%		

Table D.2A

Energy Intensity Analysis Data for the Subperiod 1977–1988: Industrial, Commercial, and Residential Sectors

State	Industrial Sector					Commercial Sector					Residential Sector				
	Raw Energy Intensity Average % Change	Residual Average % Change	Variate Average % Change	Residual Ranking	Movement	Raw Energy Intensity Average % Change	Residual Average % Change	Variate Average % Change	Residual Ranking	Movement	Raw Energy Intensity Average % Change	Residual Average % Change	Variate Average % Change	Residual Ranking	Movement
Alabama	-2.25%	-0.93%	-0.96%	17	3	-1.27%	0.75%	-0.58%	37	-7	1.08%	0.39%	2.13%	33	7
Arizona	-5.66%	-1.13%	-4.18%	13	-10	-2.87%	-1.20%	-0.23%	7	7	0.23%	-0.39%	2.06%	11	12
Arkansas	-1.63%	0.43%	-1.71%	31	-7	-2.93%	-1.08%	-0.42%	10	3	-1.46%	-1.71%	1.69%	2	1
California	-4.01%	-0.61%	-3.04%	22	-13	-3.51%	-1.13%	-0.95%	9	-3	-1.11%	0.24%	0.10%	29	-25
Colorado	-4.86%	-1.69%	-2.82%	8	-1	0.31%	1.95%	-0.20%	46	-2	0.38%	0.03%	1.79%	26	6
Connecticut	-5.63%	-2.90%	-2.38%	3	1	-3.33%	0.04%	-1.93%	26	-17	0.42%	-0.35%	2.22%	13	20
Delaware	-2.21%	-1.60%	-0.25%	9	12	-7.01%	-1.73%	-3.84%	5	-4	1.33%	0.78%	1.99%	45	-1
Florida	-6.29%	-3.23%	-2.71%	2	-1	-1.32%	1.32%	-1.21%	41	-15	0.76%	0.60%	1.60%	41	-4
Georgia	-1.12%	0.51%	-1.27%	32	-3	-2.65%	-0.20%	-1.01%	21	-5	1.17%	0.44%	2.17%	35	6
Idaho	-0.18%	2.19%	-2.01%	42	-4	-1.40%	-0.70%	0.73%	13	12	-0.06%	0.45%	0.93%	36	-21
Illinois	-0.14%	2.52%	-2.31%	43	4	-3.24%	-1.38%	-0.42%	6	4	0.09%	0.71%	0.83%	42	-23
Indiana	-1.14%	-0.50%	-0.28%	24	4	-1.12%	0.10%	0.22%	29	3	0.26%	0.28%	1.43%	30	-3
Iowa	1.92%	1.43%	0.85%	37	10	-1.74%	-1.14%	0.83%	8	14	-0.30%	-0.55%	1.69%	9	2
Kansas	-0.43%	0.92%	-1.00%	34	0	-0.71%	0.85%	-0.12%	38	1	-0.26%	-0.24%	1.42%	15	-3
Kentucky	-1.40%	0.13%	-1.18%	28	-1	-2.42%	-0.24%	-0.74%	20	-2	1.34%	0.96%	1.82%	47	-2
Louisiana	-2.15%	-1.22%	-0.58%	11	12	-2.61%	-0.62%	-0.55%	15	2	0.21%	0.18%	1.47%	27	-5
Maine	-0.54%	2.19%	-2.37%	41	-8	-1.26%	0.66%	-0.48%	32	-1	0.25%	-0.22%	1.92%	16	9
Maryland	-2.27%	-0.45%	-1.47%	25	-6	-4.08%	-2.37%	-0.27%	2	1	1.28%	0.72%	2.01%	43	0
Massachusetts	-5.23%	-2.42%	-2.45%	6	-1	-5.85%	-2.25%	-2.17%	3	-1	0.08%	-0.83%	2.35%	5	13
Michigan	-0.31%	0.77%	-0.73%	33	3	-0.91%	-0.12%	0.65%	23	13	-0.19%	-0.43%	1.68%	10	3
Minnesota	-1.45%	1.49%	-2.58%	38	-12	-1.58%	0.08%	-0.22%	27	-3	0.37%	-0.32%	2.13%	14	17
Mississippi	-0.13%	0.06%	0.17%	27	13	-1.31%	0.71%	-0.58%	36	-9	0.76%	0.01%	2.19%	25	11
Missouri	-2.96%	-1.13%	-1.47%	12	0	-2.07%	-0.39%	-0.25%	18	2	-0.62%	-0.77%	1.59%	6	0
Montana	1.13%	3.72%	-2.23%	46	0	-0.13%	0.38%	0.92%	31	11	-0.58%	-0.13%	0.99%	23	-15
Nebraska	-2.75%	-0.58%	-1.81%	23	-10	-1.02%	-0.04%	0.46%	25	9	0.33%	-0.17%	1.94%	19	11
Nevada	-2.15%	1.66%	-3.46%	40	-18	-3.57%	-2.50%	0.36%	1	4	-0.98%	-1.07%	1.53%	4	1

Table D.2A—Continued

	Industrial Sector					Commercial Sector					Residential Sector				
State	Raw Energy Intensity Average % Change	Residual Average % Change	Variate Average % Change	Residual Ranking	Move-ment	Raw Energy Intensity Average % Change	Residual Average % Change	Variate Average % Change	Residual Ranking	Move-ment	Raw Energy Intensity Average % Change	Residual Average % Change	Variate Average % Change	Residual Ranking	Move-ment
New Hampshire	-4.48%	0.03%	-4.15%	26	-18	-0.74%	2.21%	-1.51%	47	-9	0.52%	-0.15%	2.11%	20	15
New Jersey	-3.95%	-2.78%	-0.82%	4	6	-3.15%	-0.31%	-1.40%	19	-8	0.27%	-0.13%	1.85%	21	7
New Mexico	-1.48%	0.94%	-2.07%	35	-10	-0.07%	1.03%	0.34%	39	4	-0.58%	-0.77%	1.63%	7	0
New York	-5.20%	-2.72%	-2.12%	5	1	-3.45%	-1.01%	-1.00%	11	-4	0.44%	0.53%	1.35%	40	-6
North Carolina	-2.27%	-0.78%	-1.13%	20	-2	-0.26%	1.93%	-0.75%	45	-5	1.24%	0.22%	2.46%	28	14
North Dakota	10.79%	4.57%	6.58%	48	0	0.97%	1.50%	0.91%	43	3	0.90%	0.35%	1.99%	32	6
Ohio	-2.27%	-1.04%	-0.88%	15	2	-0.90%	0.35%	0.19%	30	7	0.01%	-0.13%	1.58%	22	-6
Oklahoma	-0.84%	-1.39%	0.90%	10	20	-0.21%	1.41%	-0.19%	42	-1	0.04%	0.53%	0.96%	39	-22
Oregon	0.55%	4.00%	-3.10%	47	-4	-1.30%	-0.15%	0.29%	22	6	-0.15%	0.43%	0.87%	34	-20
Pennsylvania	-2.58%	-0.84%	-1.38%	18	-2	-2.04%	-0.66%	0.06%	14	7	-0.43%	-0.72%	1.74%	8	2
Rhode Island	-5.88%	-4.39%	-1.14%	1	1	-3.07%	-0.51%	-1.12%	17	-5	1.06%	0.32%	2.18%	31	8
South Carolina	-0.77%	1.25%	-1.66%	36	-5	-3.41%	-0.59%	-1.39%	16	-8	1.60%	0.51%	2.53%	38	9
South Dakota	0.63%	-0.80%	1.78%	19	25	-2.31%	-0.99%	0.11%	12	7	0.24%	-0.21%	1.89%	17	7
Tennessee	-2.71%	-0.65%	-1.70%	21	-7	-3.86%	-1.89%	-0.53%	4	0	0.14%	-0.21%	1.79%	18	3
Texas	-0.32%	-1.05%	1.09%	14	21	-0.99%	0.70%	-0.25%	35	0	0.12%	0.46%	1.11%	37	-17
Utah	-3.52%	-0.95%	-2.22%	16	-5	-1.11%	0.09%	0.24%	28	5	-2.65%	-2.04%	0.84%	1	0
Vermont	-2.65%	0.37%	-2.66%	30	-15	-2.80%	0.67%	-2.03%	33	-18	-1.77%	-1.52%	1.19%	3	-1
Virginia	-0.27%	0.26%	-0.18%	29	8	-1.63%	0.68%	-0.88%	34	-11	1.57%	0.73%	2.28%	44	2
Washington	-0.66%	2.89%	-3.19%	44	-12	0.52%	1.74%	0.21%	44	1	-0.50%	0.91%	0.04%	46	-37
West Virginia	-0.04%	-1.75%	2.06%	7	34	1.17%	1.14%	1.47%	40	7	0.29%	-0.36%	2.10%	12	17
Wisconsin	0.29%	1.64%	-0.99%	39	3	-1.30%	-0.10%	0.24%	24	5	0.25%	-0.02%	1.71%	24	2
Wyoming	0.79%	3.55%	-2.40%	45	0	3.15%	2.99%	1.60%	48	0	2.32%	2.64%	1.12%	48	0
Statewide Average	-1.68%	0.00%	-1.33%			-1.80%	0.00%	-0.36%			0.20%	0.00%	1.65%		

Table D.2B

Energy Intensity Analysis Data for the Subperiod 1977–1988: Transportation Sector and Total Aggregate

State	Transportation Sector					Total Aggregate Energy Intensity				
	Raw Energy Intensity Average % Change	Residual Average % Change	Variate Average % Change	Residual Ranking	Move-ment	Raw Energy Intensity Average % Change	Residual Average % Change	Variate Average % Change	Residual Ranking	Move-ment
Alabama	-2.54%	-2.20%	1.71%	1	0	-2.71%	-0.34%	-2.13%	16	3
Arizona	-1.03%	-1.38%	2.40%	2	3	-3.67%	-0.38%	-3.05%	14	-6
Arkansas	-0.37%	-0.36%	2.02%	14	3	-2.83%	-0.61%	-1.98%	11	5
California	-0.39%	-0.45%	2.11%	12	4	-3.54%	-0.26%	-3.04%	20	-11
Colorado	-0.95%	-0.82%	1.92%	4	2	-2.82%	-0.13%	-2.45%	23	-6
Connecticut	0.05%	-0.23%	2.32%	17	9	-4.49%	0.36%	-4.61%	36	-32
Delaware	0.80%	0.54%	2.31%	40	6	-4.05%	-1.24%	-2.56%	1	5
Florida	0.12%	-0.09%	2.26%	23	7	-3.11%	-0.05%	-2.82%	27	-14
Georgia	0.60%	-0.05%	2.69%	24	20	-2.44%	0.84%	-3.04%	44	-22
Idaho	-1.54%	-0.53%	1.03%	8	-5	-1.46%	-0.06%	-1.16%	26	11
Illinois	-0.49%	0.05%	1.51%	30	-17	-2.74%	-0.31%	-2.19%	17	1
Indiana	0.36%	0.25%	2.14%	35	3	-1.54%	-0.63%	-0.67%	9	27
Iowa	-0.57%	0.03%	1.44%	29	-18	-0.50%	0.14%	-0.40%	31	15
Kansas	-0.19%	-0.03%	1.88%	25	-3	-1.56%	0.80%	-2.12%	43	-8
Kentucky	1.31%	1.49%	1.86%	48	-1	-1.62%	-0.24%	-1.13%	21	12
Louisiana	0.12%	1.05%	1.11%	43	-12	-2.33%	-0.79%	-1.30%	5	21
Maine	1.54%	1.23%	2.35%	45	3	-2.61%	1.28%	-3.65%	46	-26
Maryland	-0.26%	-0.65%	2.43%	5	15	-3.22%	0.13%	-3.11%	30	-19
Massachusetts	0.47%	-0.38%	2.89%	13	29	-5.39%	-0.65%	-4.51%	8	-7
Michigan	-0.57%	-0.53%	1.99%	9	1	-1.24%	-0.07%	-0.93%	24	16
Minnesota	-0.17%	-0.14%	2.01%	19	4	-2.26%	0.39%	-2.40%	38	-10
Mississippi	0.79%	1.29%	1.54%	46	-1	-0.78%	0.34%	-0.89%	35	10
Missouri	0.05%	-0.02%	2.11%	26	1	-2.43%	-0.35%	-1.84%	15	8
Montana	-0.51%	0.46%	1.07%	39	-27	-0.85%	0.60%	-1.21%	40	3
Nebraska	-0.48%	-0.27%	1.83%	15	-1	-2.07%	-0.14%	-1.69%	22	8
Nevada	-0.78%	-0.11%	1.37%	22	-15	-2.88%	-0.53%	-2.11%	12	3

Table D.2B—Continued

State	Transportation Sector					Total Aggregate Energy Intensity				
	Raw Energy Intensity Average % Change	Residual Average % Change	Variate Average % Change	Residual Ranking	Move-ment	Raw Energy Intensity Average % Change	Residual Average % Change	Variate Average % Change	Residual Ranking	Move-ment
New Hampshire	0.27%	-0.52%	2.83%	10	24	-5.02%	0.33%	-5.10%	33	-31
New Jersey	0.46%	-0.59%	3.08%	6	35	-3.20%	0.38%	-3.34%	37	-25
New Mexico	-0.31%	0.13%	1.59%	32	-14	-1.61%	0.09%	-1.46%	29	5
New York	-0.44%	-0.52%	2.12%	11	4	-4.56%	-0.93%	-3.39%	2	1
North Carolina	0.45%	0.23%	2.26%	34	6	-2.25%	0.42%	-2.43%	39	-10
North Dakota	0.10%	1.00%	1.15%	42	-14	3.27%	1.97%	1.54%	48	0
Ohio	-0.25%	0.03%	1.76%	28	-7	-2.31%	-0.48%	-1.59%	13	14
Oklahoma	-0.64%	-0.13%	1.53%	21	-13	-1.35%	-0.63%	-1.20%	10	29
Oregon	0.29%	0.71%	1.62%	41	-5	-0.79%	0.65%	-2.06%	41	3
Pennsylvania	-0.02%	0.00%	2.02%	27	-3	-3.01%	-0.71%	-3.49%	6	8
Rhode Island	0.35%	0.43%	1.96%	38	-1	-4.03%	-0.30%	-2.77%	18	-11
South Carolina	0.28%	0.29%	2.03%	37	-2	-2.34%	0.67%	-1.53%	42	-18
South Dakota	-0.58%	-0.14%	1.60%	20	-11	-1.76%	0.01%	-2.99%	28	3
Tennessee	0.11%	0.19%	1.97%	33	-4	-3.50%	-0.27%	-0.52%	19	-9
Texas	-1.78%	-1.20%	1.45%	3	-1	-1.63%	-0.87%	-1.66%	4	28
Utah	-1.19%	-0.57%	1.42%	7	-3	-2.57%	-0.67%	-4.00%	7	14
Vermont	0.37%	-0.26%	2.67%	16	23	-4.30%	-0.06%	-2.38%	25	-20
Virginia	0.17%	-0.18%	2.39%	18	14	-2.34%	0.28%	-2.48%	32	-7
Washington	0.55%	0.27%	2.32%	36	7	-1.22%	1.50%	0.19%	47	-6
West Virginia	0.23%	1.22%	1.05%	44	-11	-0.95%	-0.90%	-1.50%	3	39
Wisconsin	-0.30%	0.12%	1.62%	31	-12	-1.39%	0.34%	-1.50%	34	4
Wyoming	0.02%	1.33%	0.73%	47	-22	0.10%	1.06%	-0.72%	45	2
Statewide Average	-0.13%		1.91%			-2.33%		-2.09%		

Table D.3A

Energy Intensity Analysis Data for the Subperiod 1988–1999: Industrial, Commercial, and Residential Sectors

State	Industrial Sector					Commercial Sector					Residential Sector				
	Raw Energy Intensity Average % Change	Residual Average % Change	Variate Average % Change	Residual Ranking	Move-ment	Raw Energy Intensity Average % Change	Residual Average % Change	Variate Average % Change	Residual Ranking	Move-ment	Raw Energy Intensity Average % Change	Residual Average % Change	Variate Average % Change	Residual Ranking	Move-ment
Alabama	0.36%	-0.20%	2.15%	20	11	-0.30%	1.57%	-0.97%	45	1	0.23%	-0.12%	1.12%	20	16
Arizona	-2.84%	-1.42%	0.17%	8	-4	-2.73%	-0.95%	-0.87%	6	5	-0.22%	0.32%	0.24%	37	-17
Arkansas	3.44%	1.68%	3.34%	43	4	-2.01%	0.21%	-1.32%	35	-11	0.52%	0.54%	0.76%	44	-1
California	1.10%	0.70%	1.98%	33	5	-2.95%	-1.02%	-1.02%	5	3	-1.00%	-0.19%	-0.04%	18	-17
Colorado	0.43%	1.50%	0.52%	40	-7	-3.68%	-1.36%	-1.42%	2	0	-0.04%	0.39%	0.34%	39	-13
Connecticut	0.06%	-0.05%	1.70%	22	7	-2.40%	-0.17%	-1.32%	25	-9	0.24%	0.22%	0.79%	32	5
Delaware	1.98%	2.04%	1.41%	46	-4	-2.77%	2.53%	-4.39%	46	-36	-0.21%	-0.25%	0.81%	16	6
Florida	2.58%	1.96%	2.13%	45	-1	-2.15%	-0.56%	-0.69%	16	6	0.11%	0.65%	0.23%	46	-13
Georgia	-0.34%	-1.22%	2.46%	10	12	-2.16%	0.00%	-1.26%	29	-8	-0.28%	0.10%	0.40%	29	-12
Idaho	-2.71%	-0.51%	-0.61%	19	-14	-2.20%	-0.74%	-0.56%	12	8	0.25%	0.79%	0.24%	48	-10
Illinois	-1.74%	-1.35%	1.20%	9	2	-2.43%	-0.77%	-0.75%	11	8	-0.22%	-0.31%	0.87%	14	7
Indiana	-1.95%	0.21%	-0.57%	26	-17	-1.85%	-0.26%	-0.69%	22	4	0.03%	-0.16%	0.97%	19	10
Iowa	0.69%	0.23%	2.05%	27	8	-1.61%	0.13%	-0.84%	32	5	0.16%	0.42%	0.51%	40	-6
Kansas	-1.41%	-0.01%	0.19%	23	-9	-2.55%	-0.38%	-1.27%	20	-1	0.00%	0.03%	0.75%	24	4
Kentucky	0.03%	0.00%	1.62%	24	3	-1.28%	0.60%	-0.98%	40	-8	0.31%	0.03%	1.05%	25	16
Louisiana	-0.07%	0.26%	1.26%	28	-2	-2.40%	-0.69%	-0.80%	13	0	0.47%	0.23%	1.01%	34	8
Maine	2.55%	1.35%	2.79%	38	5	-1.33%	0.37%	-0.80%	38	4	0.53%	0.59%	0.71%	45	-1
Maryland	-4.59%	-4.75%	1.75%	1	2	2.08%	3.59%	-0.60%	48	0	-0.30%	-0.29%	0.76%	15	-1
Massachusetts	2.67%	1.38%	2.88%	39	7	-3.21%	-0.92%	-1.39%	8	-5	-0.40%	-0.66%	1.04%	2	5
Michigan	-0.18%	-0.63%	2.04%	18	6	-1.27%	1.05%	-1.42%	43	-2	-0.01%	0.00%	0.76%	23	4
Minnesota	0.99%	1.55%	1.03%	41	-4	-2.44%	-0.25%	-1.28%	23	-9	0.05%	0.09%	0.73%	28	3
Mississippi	0.95%	1.12%	1.42%	37	-1	-0.77%	0.89%	-0.76%	42	1	0.61%	0.44%	0.94%	42	3
Missouri	-0.49%	-0.74%	1.84%	17	3	-1.75%	-0.09%	-0.76%	26	2	0.18%	0.03%	0.92%	26	9
Montana	1.46%	1.71%	1.34%	44	-4	-3.15%	-1.64%	-0.61%	1	4	-0.18%	0.12%	0.48%	30	-7
Nebraska	-0.17%	0.93%	0.48%	36	-11	-3.15%	-1.19%	-1.06%	3	1	-0.11%	0.07%	0.59%	27	-3
Nevada	0.14%	2.97%	-1.25%	47	-17	-3.14%	-0.41%	-1.83%	19	-13	-0.75%	0.22%	-0.20%	33	-31

Table D.3A—Continued

State	Industrial Sector — Raw Energy Intensity Average % Change	Industrial — Residual Average % Change	Industrial — Variate Average % Change	Industrial — Residual Ranking	Industrial — Movement	Commercial Sector — Raw Energy Intensity Average % Change	Commercial — Residual Average % Change	Commercial — Variate Average % Change	Commercial — Residual Ranking	Commercial — Movement	Residential Sector — Raw Energy Intensity Average % Change	Residential — Residual Average % Change	Residential — Variate Average % Change	Residential — Residual Ranking	Residential — Movement
New Hampshire	-1.47%	-0.84%	0.95%	15	-2	-1.42%	1.16%	-1.68%	44	-9	-0.60%	-0.38%	0.56%	9	-6
New Jersey	1.81%	0.66%	2.74%	32	9	-1.85%	-0.01%	-0.93%	27	-1	-0.44%	-0.34%	0.67%	13	-7
New Mexico	-4.78%	-1.76%	-1.43%	6	-4	-1.87%	-0.79%	-0.17%	10	15	0.27%	0.39%	0.66%	38	2
New York	2.62%	1.64%	2.57%	42	3	-1.18%	0.33%	-0.61%	37	5	-0.09%	0.20%	0.49%	31	-6
North Carolina	-1.91%	-0.91%	0.59%	14	-4	-2.47%	-0.92%	-0.65%	7	6	-0.44%	-0.50%	0.84%	5	0
North Dakota	1.22%	-1.19%	4.00%	11	28	-0.56%	0.68%	-0.34%	41	4	0.86%	0.68%	0.95%	47	1
Ohio	-0.31%	0.15%	1.14%	25	-2	-2.39%	-0.19%	-1.30%	24	-6	-0.31%	-0.36%	0.83%	11	1
Oklahoma	-1.70%	0.61%	-0.72%	31	-19	-1.44%	-0.49%	-0.06%	18	16	0.26%	0.45%	0.58%	43	-4
Oregon	-6.30%	-2.20%	-2.52%	4	-3	-2.77%	-0.83%	-1.04%	9	0	-0.33%	-0.01%	0.46%	22	-12
Pennsylvania	-2.32%	-1.95%	1.22%	5	3	-1.73%	0.14%	-0.96%	33	-4	-0.26%	-0.43%	0.94%	8	10
Rhode Island	8.25%	5.03%	4.81%	48	0	-2.26%	-0.49%	-0.87%	17	2	-0.30%	-0.45%	0.92%	6	9
South Carolina	-0.48%	0.26%	0.84%	29	-8	-1.30%	0.20%	-0.59%	34	5	0.04%	-0.60%	1.41%	4	26
South Dakota	-2.42%	-3.34%	2.51%	2	4	-1.34%	0.43%	-0.87%	39	-2	-0.38%	-0.36%	0.76%	10	-2
Tennessee	-2.36%	-2.66%	1.88%	3	4	1.04%	3.37%	-1.43%	47	0	-0.30%	-0.36%	0.83%	12	1
Texas	-0.90%	0.90%	-0.21%	35	-17	-3.11%	-0.58%	-1.63%	14	-7	-0.30%	-0.06%	0.53%	21	-5
Utah	-0.53%	-1.05%	2.11%	12	7	-2.02%	0.07%	-1.19%	30	-7	0.09%	0.25%	0.61%	35	-3
Vermont	0.58%	0.83%	1.33%	34	0	-1.42%	-0.27%	-0.25%	21	15	0.75%	0.43%	1.10%	41	6
Virginia	0.38%	0.49%	1.48%	30	2	-1.66%	0.09%	-0.86%	31	-1	-0.35%	-0.65%	1.07%	3	6
Washington	-1.36%	-0.10%	0.33%	21	-6	-4.00%	-1.15%	-1.94%	4	-3	-0.56%	-0.44%	0.66%	7	-3
West Virginia	-0.97%	-1.69%	2.31%	7	10	-0.70%	-0.01%	0.21%	28	16	0.72%	0.28%	1.21%	36	10
Wisconsin	-1.03%	-0.82%	1.38%	16	0	-1.57%	0.30%	-0.97%	36	-4	-0.25%	-0.25%	0.77%	17	2
Wyoming	0.04%	-0.97%	2.60%	13	15	-1.54%	-0.57%	-0.07%	15	18	-0.33%	-0.79%	1.24%	1	10
Statewide Average	-0.23%		1.36%			-1.90%		-1.00%			-0.05%		0.73%		

Table D.3B

Energy Intensity Analysis Data for the Subperiod 1988–1999: Transportation Sector and Total Aggregate

State	Transportation Sector					Total Aggregate Energy Intensity				
	Raw Energy Intensity Average % Change	Residual Average % Change	Variate Average % Change	Residual Ranking	Move-ment	Raw Energy Intensity Average % Change	Residual Average % Change	Variate Average % Change	Residual Ranking	Move-ment
Alabama	0.15%	-0.95%	1.55%	4	7	-1.06%	0.44%	-0.75%	40	-3
Arizona	0.23%	-0.06%	0.75%	20	-7	-2.24%	-0.71%	-0.78%	4	5
Arkansas	1.33%	-0.05%	1.83%	21	13	0.44%	1.57%	-0.39%	48	0
California	-0.79%	-0.48%	0.14%	12	-10	-1.68%	-0.45%	-0.49%	12	15
Colorado	0.52%	-0.50%	1.47%	11	10	-2.54%	0.09%	-1.89%	28	-24
Connecticut	0.57%	0.80%	0.22%	44	-22	-1.91%	0.04%	-1.20%	27	-7
Delaware	-0.07%	-0.46%	0.84%	13	-5	-2.54%	0.42%	-2.22%	39	-34
Florida	-0.11%	-0.70%	1.04%	10	-3	-1.40%	-0.55%	-0.10%	10	21
Georgia	0.83%	0.14%	1.14%	27	-3	-2.12%	-0.38%	-0.99%	15	-4
Idaho	1.78%	0.59%	1.64%	40	2	-2.05%	-0.09%	-1.22%	23	-8
Illinois	1.17%	0.26%	1.35%	33	-2	-2.09%	-0.54%	-0.81%	11	2
Indiana	1.09%	-0.04%	1.58%	22	7	-2.08%	-0.13%	-1.21%	18	-4
Iowa	1.37%	-0.25%	2.07%	16	19	-1.03%	0.71%	-1.00%	44	-4
Kansas	-0.32%	-1.20%	1.33%	2	2	-2.32%	-0.74%	-0.83%	3	4
Kentucky	1.13%	-0.23%	1.81%	17	13	-1.12%	0.32%	-0.70%	37	-4
Louisiana	0.40%	-1.50%	2.34%	1	15	-1.03%	0.10%	-0.39%	29	10
Maine	0.27%	-0.37%	1.09%	14	0	-0.57%	0.26%	-0.09%	33	10
Maryland	0.43%	0.22%	0.66%	31	-14	-2.00%	-0.57%	-0.69%	9	7
Massachusetts	0.33%	0.28%	0.49%	34	-19	-1.87%	-0.12%	-1.00%	22	-1
Michigan	1.52%	0.41%	1.56%	37	1	-1.11%	-0.30%	-0.06%	16	19
Minnesota	1.85%	0.74%	1.56%	42	1	-1.12%	1.08%	-1.45%	46	-12
Mississippi	1.95%	0.44%	1.96%	38	6	-0.44%	1.12%	-0.82%	47	-3
Missouri	1.59%	0.77%	1.27%	43	-4	-1.06%	0.60%	-0.92%	43	-5
Montana	1.28%	0.07%	1.66%	25	8	-0.67%	-0.12%	0.19%	21	21
Nebraska	1.71%	0.24%	1.91%	32	8	-1.73%	-0.01%	-0.98%	25	0
Nevada	-1.03%	-0.80%	0.22%	6	-5	-1.95%	-0.05%	-1.16%	24	-6

Table D.3B—Continued

	Transportation Sector					Total Aggregate Energy Intensity				
State	Raw Energy Intensity Average % Change	Residual Average % Change	Variate Average % Change	Residual Ranking	Move-ment	Raw Energy Intensity Average % Change	Residual Average % Change	Variate Average % Change	Residual Ranking	Move-ment
New Hampshire	1.27%	1.08%	0.63%	47	-15	-1.92%	-0.13%	-1.05%	19	0
New Jersey	0.18%	0.12%	0.51%	26	-14	-2.00%	-0.59%	-0.66%	8	9
New Mexico	0.88%	0.14%	1.18%	28	-2	-2.14%	-0.25%	-1.15%	17	-7
New York	-0.12%	-0.18%	0.51%	18	-12	-1.08%	0.30%	-0.64%	36	0
North Carolina	0.43%	-0.32%	1.20%	15	3	-2.65%	-0.70%	-1.20%	5	-2
North Dakota	2.56%	0.88%	2.13%	46	1	-0.44%	0.55%	-0.25%	42	3
Ohio	0.95%	-0.09%	1.49%	19	8	-1.59%	0.30%	-1.14%	35	-7
Oklahoma	1.44%	0.15%	1.74%	29	7	-1.52%	0.24%	-1.02%	32	-3
Oregon	-0.55%	-1.02%	0.92%	3	0	-3.84%	-0.83%	-2.26%	2	-1
Pennsylvania	0.85%	0.21%	1.09%	30	-5	-2.30%	-0.43%	-1.12%	14	-6
Rhode Island	-0.06%	0.05%	0.34%	24	-15	-0.39%	0.42%	-0.07%	38	8
South Carolina	1.78%	0.83%	1.40%	45	-4	-1.42%	0.19%	-0.87%	31	-1
South Dakota	2.11%	0.46%	2.09%	39	6	-1.77%	-0.12%	-0.90%	20	4
Tennessee	0.48%	-0.79%	1.72%	8	12	-2.12%	-0.69%	-0.68%	6	6
Texas	0.03%	-0.95%	1.43%	5	5	-2.38%	0.27%	-1.91%	34	-28
Utah	0.74%	-0.80%	1.99%	7	16	-1.81%	-0.45%	-0.61%	13	10
Vermont	1.03%	0.39%	1.09%	36	-8	-0.85%	0.87%	-0.97%	45	-4
Virginia	0.47%	0.03%	0.89%	23	-4	-1.81%	0.01%	-1.08%	26	-4
Washington	-0.29%	-0.73%	0.89%	9	-4	-3.27%	-0.89%	-1.64%	1	1
West Virginia	2.18%	0.71%	1.92%	41	5	-1.28%	0.48%	-1.01%	41	-9
Wisconsin	1.47%	0.32%	1.60%	35	2	-1.69%	0.12%	-1.06%	30	-4
Wyoming	3.39%	2.12%	1.72%	48	0	-0.11%	-0.63%	1.26%	7	40
Statewide Average	0.84%		1.29%			-1.62%		-0.87%		

Bibliography

American Council for an Energy Efficient Economy, "Summer Studies on Energy Efficiency in Industry," ACEEE Industry Conference, Asilomar, Calif., August 1999 and August 2001.

Ang, B. W., "Is the Energy Intensity a Less Useful Indicator Than the Carbon Factor in the Study of Climate Change?" *Energy Policy,* Vol. 27, No. 15, December 1999, pp. 943–946.

BEA. *See* Bureau of Economic Analysis, U.S. Department of Commerce.

Berndt, E. R., and D. O. Wood, "An Economic Interpretation of the Energy-GNP Ratio," in M. S. Macrakis, ed., *Energy: Demand, Conservation and Institutional Problems,* Cambridge, Mass.: MIT Press, 1974.

Bernstein, Mark, Robert J. Lempert, David S. Loughran, and David Santana Ortiz, *The Public Benefit of California's Investments in Energy Efficiency,* Santa Monica, Calif.: RAND, MR-1212.0-CEC, 2000.

Boyd, Gale, et al., "Energy Intensity Improvements in Steel Minimills," *Contemporary Policy Issues,* Vol. 11, No. 3, 1993, pp. 88–100.

Brown, Marilyn A., Mark D. Levine, Walter Short, and Jonathan G. Koomey, "Scenarios for a Clean Energy Future," *Energy Policy,* Vol. 29, 2001, pp. 1179–1196.

Bureau of Economic Analysis, U.S. Department of Commerce, *Regional Accounts Data,* "Annual State Personal Income," Per capita disposable personal income table, n.d. (available at http://www.bea.doc.gov/bea/regional/spi/).

Bureau of Economic Analysis, U.S. Department of Commerce, *Regional Accounts Data,* "Annual State Personal Income," Population table, n.d. (available at http://www.bea.doc.gov/bea/regional/spi/).

Bureau of Economic Analysis, U.S. Department of Commerce, *Regional Accounts Data,* "Annual State Personal Income," SA25 archive, 1980–2001: Total full-time and part-time employment by industry, n.d. (available at http://www.bea.doc.gov/bea/regional/spi/).

Bureau of Economic Analysis, U.S. Department of Commerce, *Regional Accounts Data,* "Gross State Product," n.d. (available at http://www.bea.doc.gov/bea/regional/data.htm).

DeCicco, John, *Transportation Energy Trends and Issues Through 2030,* Washington, D.C.: ACEEE, December 1997.

94

Doms, Mark E., and Timothy Dunne, "Energy Intensity, Electricity Consumption, and Advanced Manufacturing Technology Usage," *Technological Forecasting and Social Change*, Elsevier, October 1995.

Dowlatabadi, Hadi, and Matthew A. Oravetz, "U.S. Long-Term Energy Intensity: Backcast and Projection," unpublished paper.

The Energy Foundation, *National Energy Policy*, "Fact Sheet: Automobile Efficiency," n.d. (available at http://www.energyfoundation.org/national/FactSheetAuto.cfm).

The Energy Foundation, *National Energy Policy*, "Fact Sheet: Industrial Energy," n.d. (available at http://www.energyfoundation.org/national/FactSheetIndustrial.cfm).

EIA. *See* Energy Information Administration.

Energy Information Administration, *Measuring Energy Efficiency in the United States' Economy: A Beginning*, Washington, D.C.: EIA, 1995.

Energy Information Administration, *Annual Energy Outlook 1999*, Washington, D.C.: EIA, 1998a.

Energy Information Administration, *United States Energy Usage and Efficiency: Measuring Changes Over Time*, Washington, D.C.: EIA, 1998b.

Energy Information Administration, *Annual Energy Outlook 2000*, Washington, D.C.: EIA, 1999.

Energy Information Administration, *Annual Energy Outlook 2001*, Washington, D.C.: EIA, 2000.

Energy Information Administration, "Energy A–Z," Table 1.9: Heating Degree Days by Census Region 1949–1999, *Annual Energy Review*, Washington, D.C.: EIA, 2001a.

Energy Information Administration, *State Energy Data Report: 1999*, May 2001b (available at http://www.eia.doe.gov/emeu/sedr/contents.html).

Energy Information Administration, *State Energy Price and Expenditure Report: 1999*, November 2001c (available at http://www.eia.doe.gov/emeu/seper/contents.html).

Eto, Joseph, *The Past, Present, and Future of U.S. Utility Demand-Side Management Programs*, Berkeley, Calif.: Lawrence Berkeley National Laboratory, LBNL-39931, 1996.

Farla, Jacco, and C. M. Blok-Kornelis, "The Quality of Energy Intensity Indicators for International Comparison in the Iron and Steel Industry," *Energy Policy*, Vol. 29, No. 7, 2001, pp. 523–543.

Freeman, Scott L., Mark J. Niefer, and Joseph M. Roop, "Measuring Industrial Energy Intensity: Practical Issues and Problems," *Energy Policy*, Vol. 25, June/July 1997, pp. 703–714.

Golove, William H., and Joseph H. Eto, *Market Barriers to Energy Efficiency: A Critical Reappraisal of the Rationale for Public Policies to Promote Energy Efficiency*, Berkeley, Calif.: Lawrence Berkeley National Laboratory, LBNL-38059, 1996.

Golove, William H., and L. J. Schipper, "Long-Term Trends in U.S. Manufacturing Energy Consumption and Carbon Dioxide Emissions," *Energy*, Vol. 21, Nos. 7 and 8, 1996, pp. 683–692.

Greene, David, and Yuehui Fan, *Transportation Energy Intensity Trends 1972–1992*, Washington, D.C.: Transportation Research Board, 1995.

Greene, David L., and Steven E. Plotkin, "Energy Futures for the U.S. Transport Sector," *Energy Policy*, Vol. 29, 2001, pp. 1255–1270.

Grissmer, David W., Ann E. Flanagan, Jennifer H. Kawata, and Stephanie Williamson, *Improving Student Achievement: What State NAEP Test Scores Tell Us*, Santa Monica, Calif.: RAND, MR-924-EDU, 2000.

Hicks, Thomas W., and Bill von Neida, *An Evaluation of America's First Energy Star Buildings: The Class of 1999*, proceedings of ACEEE summer study on energy efficiency in buildings, Asilomar, Calif., 2000.

Interlaboratory Working Group, *Scenarios for a Clean Energy Future*, Oak Ridge, Tenn.: Oak Ridge National Laboratory, and Berkeley, Calif.: Lawrence Berkeley National Laboratory, ORNL/CON-476 and LBNL-44029, 2000 (available at http://www.ornl.gov/ORNL/Energy_Eff/CEF.htm).

Interlaboratory Working Group, *Scenarios of U.S. Carbon Reductions: Potential Impacts of Energy-Efficient and Low-Carbon Technologies by 2010 and Beyond*, Berkeley, Calif.: Lawrence Berkeley National Laboratory, 2000.

International Energy Agency, *Energy Efficiency Initiative*, Vol. I, Paris, France: International Energy Agency, n.d.

International Energy Agency, *Transport, Energy, and Climate Change*, Paris, France: International Energy Agency, November 1997 (executive summary of report is available at http://www.iea.org/pubs/studies/files/transpor/transpor.htm).

International Workshop on Industrial Energy Efficiency, "Industrial Energy Efficiency: Policies and Programs," conference proceedings, Washington, D.C., May 26–27, 1994.

Koomey, John, et al., "Efficiency Improvements in U.S. Office Equipment: Expected Policy Impacts and Uncertainties," *Energy Policy*, Vol. 24, No. 12, 1996, pp. 1101–1110.

Kydes, Andy S., "Energy Intensity and Carbon Emission Responses to Technological Change: The U.S. Outlook," *Energy Journal*, Vol. 20, No. 3, 1999, pp. 93–121.

Lawrence Berkeley National Laboratory, "Exploring the Energy Efficiency Gap," Energy End-Use Forecasting Web site, Berkeley, Calif. (available at http://enduse.lbl.gov/Projects/EfficiencyGap.html).

Lemar, Paul L., "The Potential Impact of Policies to Promote Combined Heat and Power in U.S. Industry," *Energy Policy*, Vol. 29, 2001, pp. 1243–1254.

Loughran, David S., Jonathan Kulick, and Mark Bernstein, "The Impact of Demand-Side Management on Aggregate Energy Efficiency," *The Energy Journal*, forthcoming.

Margolick, Michael, and Doug Russell, Global Change Strategies International, Inc., *Corporate Greenhouse Gas Reduction Targets*, prepared for the Pew Center for Global Climate Change, November 2001 (available at http://www.pewclimate.org/projects/ghg_targets.cfm).

Martin, N., N. Anglani, M. Khurshch, D. Einstein, E. Worrell, and L. K. Price, *Opportunities to Improve Energy Efficiency and Reduce Greenhouse Gas Emissions in the U.S. Pulp and Paper Industry*, Berkeley, Calif.: Lawrence Berkeley National Laboratory, LBNL-46141, 2000.

Martin, N., E. Worrell, M. Ruth, L. Price, R. N. Elliott, A. M. Shipley, and J. Thorne, *Emerging Energy-Efficient Industrial Technologies*, Berkeley, Calif.: Lawrence Berkeley National Laboratory, LBNL-46990, 2000.

Miketa, Asami, "Analysis of Energy Intensity Developments in Manufacturing Sectors in Industrialized and Developing Countries," *Energy Policy*, Vol. 29, No. 10, 2001, pp. 769–775.

Nadel, Steven, and Howard Geller, *Energy Efficiency Policies for a Strong America*, Washington, D.C.: ACEEE, 2001.

Nadel, Steven, and Howard Geller, *Smart Energy Policies: Saving Money and Reducing Pollutant Emissions Through Greater Energy Efficiency*, Washington, D.C.: ACEEE, Report E012, September 2001.

Nadel, Steven, Leo Rainer, Michael Shepard, Margaret Suozzo, and Jennifer Thorne, *Emerging Energy-Saving Technologies and Practices for the Buildings Sector*, Washington, D.C.: ACEEE, December 1998 (executive summary of report is available at http://www.aceee.org/pubs/a985.htm).

Nagata, Yutaka, "The U.S./Japan Comparison of Energy Intensity: Estimating the Real Gap," *Energy Policy*, Vol. 25, June/July 1997, pp. 683–691.

National Energy Policy, report of the National Energy Policy Development Group, Washington, D.C.: U.S. Government Printing Office, May 2001 (available at http://www.whitehouse.gov/energy/).

Nilsson, Lars J., *Energy Intensity Trends in 31 Industrial and Developing Countries 1950–1988*, University of Lund, London, England: Pergamon Press, 1993.

Ortiz, David Santana, and Mark Bernstein, *Measures of Residential Energy Consumption and Their Relationships to DOE Policy*, Santa Monica, Calif.: RAND, MR-1105.0-DOE, 1999.

Office of Energy Efficiency and Renewable Energy, U.S. Department of Energy, *Office of Industrial Technology: Summary of Program Results*, 2000 (available at the Pacific Northwest National Laboratory Web site at http://www.pnl.gov/impacts/).

Quinlan, Patrick, Howard Geller, and Steven Nadel, *Tax Incentives for Innovative Energy-Efficient Technologies*, Washington, D.C.: ACEEE, Report E013, October 2001.

Ridker, Ronald, and William Watson, *To Choose a Future*, Baltimore, Md.: Johns Hopkins University Press, 1980.

Ross, Marc, "Improving the Efficiency of Electricity Use in Manufacturing," *Science*, Vol. 244, April 1989, pp. 311–317.

Schipper, Lee, *Indicators of Energy Use and Efficiency*, Paris, France: International Energy Agency, 1997.

Schipper, Lee, and Richard B. Howarth, "United States Energy Use from 1973 to 1987: The Impacts of Improved Efficiency," *Annual Review of Energy*, Vol. 15, 1990, pp. 455–504.

Schipper, Lee, and Scott Murtishaw, "Disaggregated Analysis of U.S. Energy Consumption in the 1990s: Evidence of the Effects of the Internet and Rapid Economic Growth," *Energy Policy*, Vol. 29, 2001, pp. 1335–1356.

Schurr, S. H., "Energy Efficiency and Economic Efficiency: An Historical Perspective," in S. H. Schurr, S. Sonenblum, and D. O. Wood, eds., *Energy, Productivity and Economic Growth*, Cambridge, Mass.: Oelgeschlager, Gunn and Hain, 1983.

Sissine, Fred J., *Energy Efficiency: A New National Outlook?* Washington, D.C.: Congressional Research Service, Report No. IB95085, 1996.

Theriault, Louis, and Ram Sahi, "Energy Intensity in the Manufacturing Sector: Canadian and International Perspective," *Energy Policy*, Vol. 25, June/July 1997, pp. 773–779.

U.S. Census Bureau, *Annual Survey of Manufacturers*, "Table 1 (New Capital Expenditures)," various years.

U.S. Census Bureau, Annual Survey of Manufacturers Web site (http://www.census.gov/econ/www/ma0300.html).

U.S. Census Bureau, Population Estimates Program, "Household and Housing Unit," n.d. (available at http://eire.census.gov/popest/archives/1990.php?PHPSESSID=e77997aa48cd59521f437598914df344#household).

U.S. Senate, *Energy Policy Act of 2002*, Senate Bill 1766, 2001.

Varone, Frédéric, and Bernard Aebischer, "Energy Efficiency: The Challenges of Policy Design," *Energy Policy*, Vol. 29, 2001, pp. 615–629.

Webber, C. A., R. E. Brown, and J. G. Koomey, "Savings Estimates for the EnergyStar Voluntary Labeling Program," *Energy Policy*, Vol. 28, 2000, pp. 1137–1149.

98

Worrell, Ernst, and Lynn Price, "Policy Scenarios for Energy Efficiency Improvement in Industry," *Energy Policy*, Vol. 29, 2001, pp. 1223–1241.

Worrell, Ernst, Lynn Price, and Nathan Martin, "Energy Efficiency and Carbon Dioxide Emissions Reduction Opportunities in the U.S. Iron and Steel Sector," *Energy*, Vol. 26, No. 5, 2001, pp. 513–536.

Worrell, Ernst, Lynn Price, and Nathan Martin, "Energy Intensity in the Iron and Steel Industry: A Comparison of Physical and Economic Indicators," *Energy Policy*, Vol. 25, June/July 1997, pp. 727–744.

Worrell, Ernst, Nathan Martin, and Lynn Price, "Potentials for Energy Efficiency Improvement in the U.S. Cement Industry," *Energy*, Vol. 25, No. 12, 2000, pp. 1189–1214.

Worrell, E., R. van Berkel, Z. Fengqi, C. Menke, R. Schaeffer, and R. O. Williams, "Technology Transfer of Energy Efficient Technologies in Industry: A Review of Trends and Policy Issues," *Energy Policy*, Vol. 29, 2001, pp. 29–43.